vegetarian
hassle free
gluten
free

Jane Devonshire

To my wonderful children Sam, Rebecca, Harry & Ben. I could not be prouder of you all. I love you loads.

Mum xxxx

vegetarian
hassle free
gluten
free

Jane Devonshire

In association with Coeliac UK

with photography by
Mike Cooper

BLOOMSBURY ABSOLUTE
LONDON · OXFORD · NEW YORK · NEW DELHI · SYDNEY

vegetarian hassle free, **gluten free**

introduction

Winning *MasterChef* certainly changed my life. My passion for cooking has become my job and I love it. I write my recipes from my heart and in this, my second book, I really wanted to reflect how we as a family have changed our diet to include more vegetarian food. It was not really a conscious choice, but more of a natural evolution in our eating habits.

Those who will have bought and read my first book, *Hassle Free, Gluten Free*, will know that my cooking of gluten-free food was sparked by my youngest son, Ben, who was diagnosed with coeliac disease when he was two years old. As the youngest of my four children, I made it my mission to feed my family as inclusively as possible. Why cook something different for Ben, when I could cook one delicious dish for everyone? So, if my first book was inspired by Ben, then this one has my daughter Rebecca in mind.

Yes, our eating habits have evolved over time and as a nation we're all eating less meat, but my love of cooking vegetarian food was primarily sparked by our daughter Rebecca becoming vegetarian whilst she was at university. I fully understood and supported her reasons, most of her friends are vegan and it became apparent that I had to expand my cooking to include vegetables as a hero, not just a wonderful side to whatever meat or fish I was cooking.

Once she turned vegetarian, Rebecca faced very similar struggles as Ben. When she went out to restaurants, there was often just one lacklustre vegetarian meal on the menu, as an afterthought, with no real thought put into it. In big cities like Manchester and London there was usually less of a problem, but smaller venues often presented a challenge. Couple that with the necessity to eat gluten-free food and we were back to square one when it came to eating out as a family.

As a chef new to the business, work has also pushed me to think more about vegetarian and vegan food; indeed every job I get asked to do has to include these options to ensure there really is something for everyone. I really enjoy finding ways to make these dishes as interesting and as filling as the more traditional meals that we plan, which tend to have meat or fish incorporated.

I was not a complete novice to creating vegetarian dishes, though. Many plant-based dinners, including the beloved Three Cheese and Mushroom Lasagne on page 57, had long been on the menu at home and at work, but I wanted to expand my repertoire and incorporate it into our everyday lives.

I am, and always have been, a lover of vegetables. My dad grows the very best veggies in his garden in London. No grass in the garden for us as kids; just neat rows of vegetables that fed us all year round. There really is nothing quite like harvesting something and cooking it within minutes, and carrots, for example, are transformed so easily. I'm sure it's because the kids worked with Grandad in the garden I never had a problem getting them to eat their greens; it's such a treat to eat what you grow. I admit to being pretty awful at gardening. I love to cook the produce but my father's talent bypassed me. We do, however, grow some things for the kitchen. We always have fresh herbs growing; basil, coriander, parsley, thyme and mint – I find them such a great way to perk any dish that is looking a little sad. Onions, carrots, runner beans, kale, tomatoes and potatoes are also currently flourishing in the garden, although the lettuce and some other salad vegetables are looking a little sad. I am persevering, though it's sometimes a battle with the chickens and other birds and wildlife. The thought of fresh vegetables straight out of the garden keeps me going. I don't think I will ever have dad's passion, but I do try.

I had never really, until *MasterChef* and Rebecca, thought about making this much-loved food a central part of my meals day-to-day; I find it strange to think that now. Why did it never cross my consciousness to make more vegetarian food at home day to day? Maybe my mind was rooted in the way I was brought up; my mum is a brilliant cook but I suppose like a lot of families in the 1970s and 80s, it was very traditional food where protein always formed the central part of the dish. But I do love a challenge and a cooking challenge is even better!

Gradually, because I was creating and testing recipes for work and feeding everyone those vegetarian dishes at home (I hate food waste) they naturally worked their way onto our regular menu. Things became much-loved and certain dishes often requested by the kids (such as the Mexican Night In on page 84, or Oven-topped Deep Pizza Pie on page 63). I was not cooking vegetarian gluten-free food; I was just cooking lovely food for the family. It didn't need a label and that to me is what is important.

There are of course other considerations that impact the way we eat. One of my great joys over the last few years has been working with Coeliac UK. I am so very proud to be an Ambassador for the charity, who support thousands of people who need to live gluten free through their information, campaigns and research. They are a lifeline to many families like ours, and make getting to grips with the gluten free diet a whole lot less daunting. You can read more about the charity on pages 220–221.

However, as gluten free families, we face unique problems which I have often spoken about in the past, and one of the biggest is how to control the cost. Living life gluten free can be prohibitively expensive, with staples like bread and pasta sometimes being three or four times the cost of their gluten counterparts. Children's cereal is exorbitant and treats invariably double the price. Eating a vegetarian meal a few times a week can genuinely reduce the cost of living for many families, whilst still supplying great nutrition.

I have tried hard in this book to reflect our style of eating and give you good, no fuss recipes that can be easily achieved at home. It's important

introduction

to me that the ingredients I cook with can be very easily sourced in local supermarkets or online with little fuss.

I am particularly proud of the doughs and pastry chapter as I know this is an area of particular importance when trying to make gluten-free food. I use Shipton Mill flour for my baking which I order online in catering bags and is delivered very quickly, but I do try to test my recipes with a number of different gluten free brands to make them work for everyone.

I have always stated that I think food should be inclusive and that includes dietary choice as well as necessity. There is something so upsetting about people being excluded from one of life's ultimate pleasures; sharing food and the experience of eating together is such a joy. I have seen first-hand with Ben how food can also exclude, and I firmly believe it shouldn't still be happening and it's definitely not happening in my kitchen, at home with my family and friends.

It's so much easier to just cook one big plate of food for the family, especially if you are cooking every day. And if that dish can easily stand alone or alongside protein-based dishes, it makes life simpler, easier and more inclusive for everyone and of course there is less washing up which is always a bonus!

This book is about my love of what I am cooking now. It reflects, like many families, how our diet is adapting to the needs and wants of different members of our family. It's full of some of my very favourite dishes; they just happen to be gluten free and vegetarian. They work brilliantly as standalone dishes but some of them equally well as accompaniments for those within your family who don't want to give up the meat or fish, or are brilliant when mixed and matched to create a veggie feast. I hope you all find them as delicious as I do.

Enjoy and happy cooking!

Jane x

a note on gluten cross-contamination

When you're maintaining a strict gluten-free diet you need to make sure you don't contaminate gluten-free food with any crumbs of food that contain gluten.

When you're cooking at home, whether for yourself or for your family and friends, here are some simple steps to follow that will help keep food preparation safe:

- Wash down surfaces before preparing food
- Cook gluten-free foods and foods that contain gluten in separate pans with separate utensils
- Standard washing up or using a dishwasher will remove gluten
- Washing up liquids are fine to use and standard rinsing will remove any traces of gluten
- You do not need to use separate cloths or sponges
- You may want to get separate bread boards to keep gluten-free and gluten-containing breads separate
- Use a separate toaster or toaster bags for gluten-free bread
- Use clean oil or a separate fryer for frying gluten-free foods
- Use different butter knives and jam spoons to prevent breadcrumbs from getting into condiments.

a note on ingredients

Where we know it's important that an ingredient is labelled gluten free, we have stated this in the recipe, such as ***gluten-free** flour*. For other ingredients which may not be labelled gluten free but which do not typically contain gluten we have put the symbol ○ against it, to remind you to double check the packaging to make sure gluten (wheat, barley, rye, oats) is not listed in the ingredients list or allergen statements.

breakfast, snacks and small plates

Gluten-free Granola

14

serves 12

I find breakfast one of the hardest meals to cater for gluten free. This granola is easy to do and a bit different, and you can add your favourite ingredients into the mix. I have deliberately avoided coconut in this mix. It's not a favourite in my house, and I find it quite overpowers the other flavours; however if you love it please feel free to add.

150g **gluten-free** rolled oats
○ 100g flaked quinoa
○ 50g puffed quinoa
1½ tablespoons ground mixed spice
½ tablespoon ground ginger
good pinch of Maldon sea salt
100g blanched hazelnuts,
  roughly crushed
150g good runny honey (I use Greek)
4 tablespoons sunflower oil
100g mixed seeds, sesame, pumpkin,
  sunflower and golden linseed
250g dried fruit; most fruit works
  but I use a mix of dried cranberries,
  sour cherries, blueberries and
  raisins; apricots and figs work
  well too

My Tip
Not all coeliacs can cope with oats, although they are a recommended part of the diet if possible. When avoiding oats, I substitute more flaked quinoa, with some added nuts for texture.

Preheat the oven to 180 °C/160°C Fan/Gas Mark 4. Line two baking trays with greaseproof paper.

In a bowl, combine the oats, flaked and puffed quinoa, mixed spice, ginger, salt and hazelnuts.

Put the honey and oil into a saucepan and bring to the boil. Stir in the dry ingredients until completely coated. Spread the mixture onto the lined baking trays and bake for 20–25 minutes, until toasted and golden.

Divide the mixed seeds and dried fruit between the baking trays and scatter them over the mixture. Push them down to mix in, pressing hard so that the mixture clumps. Leave to cool.

The cooled granola can be stored in an airtight jar for 2–3 weeks. I like to serve it with Greek set yoghurt and runny honey.

Breakfast Waffles

makes 4
large waffles

Breakfast is a dish we struggle with. Ben gets bored of the same old cereals and to be honest they don't seem very filling and are often full of sugars and preservatives. We are lucky he can tolerate oats but porridge every day is still pretty bland, according to Ben. So last year I invested in a waffle maker. Mine cost just over £20 online and is a great addition to the kitchen. We use this waffle batter to make breakfasts and brunches with lots of different toppings, especially at the weekend.

250g **gluten-free** plain flour
2½ teaspoons **gluten-free** baking
  powder
2 tablespoons caster sugar
½ teaspoon xanthan gum
½ teaspoon sea salt
2 large eggs, separated
350ml milk
80g unsalted butter, melted
½ teaspoon vanilla bean paste (omit
  if making a savoury topping)
flavourless oil, for spraying

You will need
waffle maker

In a large bowl, combine the flour, baking powder, sugar, xanthan gum and salt.

Whisk the egg whites until they form stiff peaks.

Add the egg yolks, milk, butter and vanilla bean paste to the dry ingredients and mix in thoroughly, until you have a wet batter.

Using your whisk or stand mixer, gently pour the batter into the whipped egg whites until it's all incorporated. Leave to stand for 5 minutes while you heat your waffle maker and gently spray it with a flavourless oil.

Fill the moulds with batter (for ease of pouring I put it into a jug first) and leave to cook for 3–5 minutes, until the waffles are golden and crispy.

You may need to cook the waffles in batches, spraying the waffle maker lightly with oil every time, until the mixture is used up. Place the finished waffles on a wire rack or put them in a low oven to keep them crispy.

My Tip
We love these with bananas, chocolate and cream, stacked and drizzled with maple syrup or agave, but they go well with any fruit or try them with the HFC (page 31). Or, for the meat eaters, these are great with crispy bacon or fried chicken. Just go wild.

Fluffy Vegan Pancakes with Apricot Compote

makes 6
pancakes

Who doesn't love pancakes? I have spent many hours of my life cooking them for what seemed like hordes of kids and adults. These vegan versions use an aquafaba meringue base to keep them light and fluffy, but I promise that they are well worth that extra bit of effort. I have included a more adult version for dessert or a boozy brunch, but please feel free to dust the pancakes with icing sugar and cover with fruit, maple syrup or cream whatever takes your fancy.

For the apricot compote topping
1 x 440g can of apricot halves in
    syrup, drained and juice reserved
2 tablespoons apricot brandy (or
    1 tablespoon normal brandy)
2 tablespoons golden caster sugar
squeeze of lemon juice
2 tablespoons coconut cream
½ teaspoon vanilla bean extract

For the pancakes
1 x 400g can chickpeas, drained
    (keep the aquafaba and reserve the
    chickpeas for use in another recipe
    or the Roasted Chickpea Snack
    on page 22)
½ teaspoon cream of tartar
2 tablespoons icing sugar, sifted, plus
    1 teaspoon
2 tablespoons **gluten-free** oat milk,
    or similar plant-based milk
15g vegan butter, softened
1 teaspoon vanilla bean paste
½ teaspoon **gluten-free** baking
    powder
75g **gluten-free** plain flour
sunflower oil, for cooking

First make the topping. Place the juice from the can of apricots into a pan with the brandy, 1 tablespoon of the sugar and the lemon juice. Simmer for about 5 minutes over a low heat until the mixture has reduced and is a light golden-coloured syrup that coats the back of the spoon. Allow to cool and set aside.

Whip the coconut cream to soft peaks with the remaining tablespoon of caster sugar and the vanilla bean extract. Set aside.

Now make the pancakes. Whisk the aquafaba until it forms stiff peaks. This will take a little longer than traditional meringue but persevere. You can easily see when it's whipped enough by holding the bowl over your head and if you don't end up with the proverbial egg on your face, it's ready, otherwise keep whisking.

Add in the cream of tartar and the sifted icing sugar and whisk for another 2 minutes until the meringue is lovely and glossy.

In a separate bowl combine the remaining ingredients for the pancakes, except the oil, and whisk until no lumps remain.

Add the aquafaba mixture to the batter, a tablespoon at a time, whisking until it's all combined.

Dip a piece of kitchen towel into the sunflower oil (don't use butter – it will burn) and wipe it around your frying pan. Heat the oil to the lowest setting on your gas or electric ring.

To serve
icing sugar, to dust (optional)

You will need
*large non-stick frying pan
    with a lid*

Add about 1½ heaped tablespoon of the mixture to the pan, to form a good sized pancake. They will spread a little and you should be able to cook two or three pancakes at a time.

Cover with a lid and leave without agitating or moving for 2–3 minutes, you should see the edges turning golden, then using two spatulas gently turn the pancakes. They are quite fragile so be careful. Once turned, cook for a further 2–3 minutes until golden brown and fluffy and remove.

To serve, gently fold about half the syrup into the coconut cream so that it forms swirls. Drizzle the rest of the syrup over the pancakes with some of the apricot halves. Spoon on the cream, dust with icing sugar, if using, and eat straight away.

Mashed Edamame Beans and Tomato Bruschetta

serves 6–8

Bruschetta make great starters and brunch dishes. These are a little special; I have used them in menu design for a couple of jobs in London recently and they have gone down a storm. The edamame bean mash can be frozen and used another time if you need to.

2 garlic cloves
200g edamame beans
good pinch of sea salt
1–2 tablespoons lemon juice
25–35ml extra-virgin olive oil

For the tomatoes
8 tomatoes (I prefer them on the
    vine for flavour)
1 banana shallot, finely chopped
10g fresh basil, chopped
½ garlic clove, finely grated
olive oil, to taste
lemon juice, to taste
sea salt, to taste

To serve
gluten-free focaccia or other good
    gluten-free bread (such as the
    French Bread on page 183), thinly
    sliced and lightly toasted
chilli oil (optional)
pea shoots (optional)

My Tip
I buy frozen peeled edamame beans from the supermarket; most supermarkets do them online. You can use broad beans but I've found they rarely come peeled and picking the skins off is very time consuming.

Place the peeled garlic cloves in a pan of cold water and bring to the boil. Plunge the beans in and blanch for a few minutes. Remove from the heat, drain and plunge the garlic and beans into a bowl of iced water.

Put the beans and garlic cloves into a food processor with the salt, lemon juice and olive oil. Pulse until it comes together but leave textured – it should not be a smooth purée. Chill and reserve.

Chop the tomatoes finely and place them in a bowl with the shallots, basil, garlic, olive oil, lemon juice and salt. Leave for at least an hour, or overnight, to infuse the flavours.

To serve, lightly toast the bread. Place a thick spread of the bean purée on top, and spoon over the chopped tomato. Liberally cover with chilli oil, and pea shoots, if using. Serve immediately.

Roasted Chickpea Snack with Smoked Paprika

serves 4–6

I love snacking. I particularly enjoy savoury snacks and am always on the lookout for something tasty which is not quite as bad for me as a bag of crisps. These chickpeas are incredibly easy to do, and they use up any leftovers I have from making one of the aquafaba meringue recipes on pages 18, 144 and 157. I throw them in the oven at the same time as the meringues and get a two-in-one result. Perfect in my house.

1 x 400g can of chickpeas, drained
½ teaspoon sea salt
1 teaspoon smoked paprika (hot or sweet depending on your taste)

Preheat the oven to 150°C/130°C Fan/Gas Mark 2.

Dry the drained chickpeas really well between two pieces of kitchen towel. If the skins come off that's good. The best results are when you peel the chickpeas; however, I've found that's really not necessary.

Sprinkle on the salt and smoked paprika and rub the chickpeas in to coat. Place on a baking tray in the oven for 1 hour.

Remove from the oven, check the seasoning and serve.

You can keep these in an airtight jar for up to a week if they are dried out completely.

My Tip
I change the flavourings on these to suit. They are great tossed in Ras El Hanout or garam masala for instance; or you could use curry powder (just check that it's gluten free).

Loaded Fries

serves 2–4

In our house we have a night, usually Friday or Saturday, where we are in our PJs and watching films. This is definitely not a healthy evening. Pizza is perfect for these nights but so are these oven-baked loaded fries. Oozing cheese and garlicky goodness they are satisfying in that wonderful comforting way that you need on those evenings.

For the tray bake

1 large potato (about 300g; King Edwards are good), cut into large chips or wedges

1 large sweet potato (about 300g), cut into large chips or wedges

2 red onions, peeled and cut into wedges

6 garlic cloves, skins left on

1 tablespoon mixed dried herbs

½ tablespoon garlic salt

2 tablespoons vegetarian Italian hard cheese

good grind of black pepper

2 tablespoons sunflower oil

125g ready-grated mozzarella cheese

For the sauce

1 x 400g can tomatoes

1 tablespoon olive oil

1 tablespoon dried mixed herbs

½ teaspoon sea salt

½ teaspoon sugar

Preheat the oven to 180°C/160°C Fan/Gas Mark 4.

Put all the tray bake ingredients except the mozzarella into an oven tray and toss them together so that the potatoes are covered by the other ingredients. Place in the oven for about 30 minutes, then turn the potatoes over and cook for a further 20–25 minutes, until golden.

Place the sauce ingredients in a saucepan and simmer until you have a thick sauce, about 5 minutes, stirring to make sure the sauce does not catch.

Remove the tray bake from the oven and take out the garlic cloves. Squish them with a fork, squeezing out all the lovely roasted garlic, and discard the skins. Toss the potatoes with the roasted garlic.

Put the potatoes in a small pile in the roasting tray and sprinkle over the mozzarella. Return to the oven and cook for another 5–7 minutes, until the cheese is golden and bubbling.

To serve, with large spoons pick up the pile, place on a plate or bowl and cover with the tomato sauce.

My Tip
I often add extra bits to this. You can use anything that works with pizza, really — we love mushrooms and olives but go crazy, it's a feast. I don't peel the potatoes, just wash them and make sure they are very dry before roasting.

Mozzarella Sticks

makes about 24
mozzarella sticks

Who doesn't love fried cheese? A total indulgence but sometimes a must have. These are lovely served with a spicy dip. We love them with the Chilli-spiced Roast Tomato and Red Pepper Dip (page 209), but a good shop-bought sweet chilli sauce is also great. Please don't be tempted to use good mozzarella for this recipe. It won't work. The cheap harder block is perfect.

*150g **gluten-free** white rice flour*
6 large eggs, beaten
*150g **gluten-free** breadcrumbs*
1 tablespoon garlic salt
1 tablespoon mixed dried herbs
1 x 400g block mozzarella, cut into
* batons about 1.5cm thick*
sunflower oil, for frying

Before you start to cook, put the rice flour, beaten eggs and breadcrumbs into separate dishes.

Season the breadcrumbs with the garlic salt and mixed dried herbs and combine thoroughly.

My Tip
You can add extra dry spices into the breadcrumbs. I like smoked paprika and have experimented with curry powder too. Just have fun with what you fancy.

Lay a large sheet of greaseproof paper onto a baking tray. Cut the mozzarella into batons.

In batches of up to six, dip the mozzarella batons into the rice flour, then into the beaten egg, then into the rice flour, then into the beaten egg again. Then roll in the breadcrumbs until thoroughly coated, making sure all the cheese is covered. You can place these in the fridge for a day if you need to.

Fill a heavy-based pan one-third full with oil and heat to a temperature of 180°C. If you don't have a thermometer, simply drop a cube of gluten-free bread into the pan; if it sinks then rises, sizzling, your oil is hot enough. Alternatively, use a deep fat fryer.

Fry in batches for 2–3 minutes, until crispy and golden and the cheese is melted. Place onto kitchen towel and serve immediately with a dip, being careful not to burn your mouth.

Vegetarian
Sausage Rolls

makes 16
snack-sized
sausage rolls

Sometimes I get a lightbulb moment and making the sausage for the vegetarian sausage roll was one of those. I wanted to make something that had the texture and flavour of a real sausage, not of the vegetable or cheese, and I think I got there. I didn't want to use meat substitutes in this book but I have used traditional proteins from Asia, tempeh being one of those. I bought some jars quite cheaply online and then set about using them. I think it's the closest to a meat texture I have found and can be blitzed to look like sausagemeat. I am really happy with these sausage rolls and they are genuinely very easy to make. The instructions below are for cocktail sausage rolls but you can make any size you like.

1 onion, finely chopped
4–5 sage leaves, chopped
splash of sunflower oil
1 jar of tempeh, drained weight 240g
1 teaspoon sea salt
good grind of black pepper
1 large egg
*30g good **gluten-free** breadcrumbs
(I use Mrs Crimble's)*
*1 x quantity of Rough Puff and
Flaky Pastry (page 196), or 1
pack of **gluten-free** ready-made
(there is less pastry in the ready-
made roll)*
1 large egg, beaten, to egg wash

Preheat the oven to 220°C/200°C Fan/Gas Mark 7. Gently fry off the onion and sage in the oil for about 5 minutes, until softened and cooked through.

Pulse-blend the drained tempeh until it has the texture of traditional sausage meat. Add the cooked onion and sage and the salt, black pepper, egg and breadcrumbs to the tempeh and stir through thoroughly.

Roll out your pastry and cut it into two strips, about 26–28cm long and 9–10cm wide. On a lightly floured board, gently roll out the filling mixture to about the size of a normal sausage and place it on the pastry, slightly off centre. Repeat, joining the rolls of filling together into one long roll, until you have nearly reached the end of each pastry strip. Egg wash along one long edge of the pastry and fold over gently, pressing to make a tight seal.

Using a sharp knife, cut through each roll every 3–4cm, to make cocktail sausage rolls. Make two slashes in the top of each sausage roll through the pastry to the sausage meat. Egg wash and place in the oven for about 20 minutes, until golden and risen.

My Tip
You can make these really herby or spicy depending on what you like best. Personally, I love brushing the inside of the pastry with gluten-free yeast extract and mixing some vegetarian Italian hard cheese into the sausage mixture for something quite different.

Spaghetti Frittata

serves 4–6

I hope I am not the only person who always makes far too much pasta; I now do it on purpose so that I can make this recipe. It makes a great lunch or light dinner with a salad but it's also fab in picnics and school lunches. You can make it in smaller individual portions if you want – muffin tins are ideal for this. It's also the perfect recipe for students; you can literally throw almost anything in to use up leftovers and make a cost-effective meal that will work both warm and cold.

3 shallots, chopped
30g unsalted butter, plus extra for greasing
2 tablespoons oil from a jar of sun-dried tomatoes
*400g cold **gluten-free** spaghetti, cooked according to the packet instructions and drained*
5–6 spring onions, including the green parts, chopped
125g sun-dried tomatoes, chopped
50g olives, chopped
20g chopped basil, stalks included
175g crumbled feta cheese, plus 50g for topping
75g strong Cheddar cheese, grated, plus 25g for topping
6 large eggs, beaten
100ml milk
good grind of black pepper
½ teaspoon garlic salt, or sea salt if preferred

You will need
baking tray or dish like a lasagne dish, about 20 x 28cm

Preheat the oven 220°C/200°C Fan/Gas Mark 7. Grease the dish with butter.

Fry off the shallots in the 30g butter and sun-dried tomato oil for 2–3 minutes, until softened and cooked through.

Place the spaghetti, spring onions, tomatoes, olives, basil and the cheeses in a large bowl, along with the cooked shallot and cooking oils, and combine well. Add the eggs and milk and incorporate well. You really want the ingredients evenly distributed throughout the pasta. Season well with black pepper and garlic salt, or sea salt if preferred.

Put the pasta mixture on the baking tray or in the dish and sprinkle on the remaining feta and Cheddar. Place in the oven and cook for 25–30 minutes, until the top is golden, the cheese is melted and the egg is set well.

Remove and leave to cool for 10 minutes before serving with a big salad.

My Tips
Once cooked and drained, just lightly toss the spaghetti you want to use in olive oil or butter to stop it sticking.

Add chilli or garlic for an extra kick. I love recipes that you can make your own so please feel free to add in whatever ingredients you like – just experiment.

Mini Pea Pasties

I found that one of the hardest things to get right day after day was lunches, as we needed things Ben could take to school or college that were easy to eat and that were not going to disintegrate or stand out as being different. These little pasties are perfect.

To be honest, I often make them with ready-made gluten-free puff pastry for ease – although they are lovely made with the Rough Puff and Flaky Pastry (page 196).

For the filling

25g unsalted butter (or 1 tablespoon
*   sunflower oil)*
1 onion, finely chopped
1 teaspoon garam masala
175g cooked frozen peas
125g mashed potato
squeeze of lemon
sea salt and black pepper

For the pastry

*1 sheet of frozen **gluten-free** puff*
*   pastry*
1 egg, beaten, to egg wash

Preheat the oven to 220°C/200° Fan/Gas Mark 7. Place the butter or oil in a large frying pan, add the onion and garam masala and cook slowly over a low heat for about 3 minutes, until the onion is softened and cooked. Remove from the heat.

Put the peas and the potato mash into the onion mix and combine thoroughly; you need to make sure all the mash is coating the peas and onion. Don't worry if you break up a few peas; the mash helps bind the mixture as well as bulk it out.

Season with a squeeze of lemon juice and with salt and a good grind of black pepper to taste.

Roll out the pastry onto a floured surface and cut into six equal squares. Section them off, but leave them in place. Then gently mark each square diagonally from corner to corner.

Place one tablespoon of the filling mix into one half of the triangle on the square. Egg wash around the inside edges and fold over the square to make a triangle pasty shape. Using a fork, gently push the edges together.

My Tip
If you don't need all the pasties at once, just wrap any you don't need in cling film and freeze them at this stage. Take them out of the freezer the night before you need them and cook them as follows.

Egg wash the top and, using the tip of a knife, just make a small incision in the top of each pasty. Transfer to a baking tray lined with greaseproof paper, and place in the oven for about 15–18 minutes, until risen and golden. Remove and eat warm or save to wrap up for lunches.

HFC – Hampshire Fried Cauliflower with a **Green Sriracha Salsa**

serves 6–8

I love this dish. It's packed full of flavour and a real favourite to serve as a starter or brunch dish. It's Rebecca's go-to when she is craving the spice of a very well-known fried chicken dish.

1 medium cauliflower, cut into florets
(approx. 400g)
3 tablespoons cornflour
100ml buttermilk
1 large egg
1 teaspoon garlic salt
½ tablespoon smoked paprika
4 tablespoons mixed herbs
sunflower oil, for frying
green chilli (optional)

For the green sriracha salsa
200g Sicilian tiger plum
tomatoes (baby)
30g coriander leaf, picked
and finely chopped
125g extra-virgin olive oil
2 tablespoons lemon juice
couple of large splashes of green
sriracha (I like it very spicy so we
add a lot, but it can be adjusted
for heat levels to taste)
good pinch of sea salt

To garnish
1 coriander leaf, finely chopped
1 green chill, finely chopped
(optional)

To make the salsa, cut the tomatoes into quarters (I like to leave the skin on), then combine with the rest of the ingredients and reserve.

Blanch the cauliflower florets in boiling water for 2–3 minutes. Drain and place on a clean tea towel or J-cloth until completely dry.

Place the cornflour and buttermilk in a large bowl, stirring well to ensure that there are no lumps, then beat in the egg. Add the garlic salt, paprika, mixed herbs and chilli, if using, and combine well.

Fill a heavy-based pan one-third full with sunflower oil and heat to 180°C. If you don't have a thermometer, simply drop a little of the batter into the pan – if it sinks then rises, sizzling, your oil is hot enough. Alternatively, use a deep fat fryer.

Dip the florets into the batter and deep fry for 3–5 minutes, until dark golden in colour and crispy. Remove and place on a kitchen towel or clean J-cloth to drain.

Serve immediately with the green sriracha salsa.

My Tip
If you don't have or can't get buttermilk, combine 1 teaspoon lemon juice with 100ml milk and leave to stand in a warm place for 15 minutes.

Onion and Potato Bhajis with Ras El Hanout Cauliflower Purée

makes 6–8 bhajis

I have always loved cauliflower, but it's only in the last few years that I have really been inspired to experiment with it– and what a fantastic vegetable it is, so versatile and full of flavour. This recipe gives quite spectacular results and you can serve it as a side or a main.

For the bhajis
200–225g potato (King Edwards
  or similar), cut into small chunks
  less than 1cm² (they don't have to
  be exact)
50g spring onion, finely sliced and
  green tops included, plus extra for
  garnishing
½ teaspoon turmeric
1 teaspoon Ras El Hanout
  spice mix
½ teaspoon chilli powder
pinch of sea salt
5–6 tablespoons gram flour
½ teaspoon lemon juice
sunflower oil, for frying

For the cauliflower purée
300g cauliflower florets
1 garlic clove
25g unsalted butter
1 teaspoon Ras El Hanout
  spice mix
50ml double cream
lemon juice, to taste
sea salt, to taste

To garnish (optional)
1 fresh red chilli, sliced
handful of spring onions, chopped

Place the potato chunks into a pan of boiling water and simmer for about 3–5 minutes, until they are tender but still retain their shape. Drain and rinse thoroughly with cold water. Allow to cool.

To make the purée, put the cauliflower and garlic into a pan of boiling water and cook until the cauliflower is tender; the time required will depend on the size of your florets but the cauliflower must be very tender with no resistance when pierced with a knife. But don't be tempted to boil it to mush. Drain, reserving some of the cooking juice.

In a small saucepan melt the butter until gently foaming and add the teaspoon of Ras El Hanout. Let it cook for 1 minute then, using a spatula, scrape it into a bowl with the cooked cauliflower and garlic clove, and the double cream. Blend until you have a smooth purée; you may need some of the cooking liquid to bring it together. Keep blending until you have a velvety smooth purée. Once you are happy with the texture, add a squeeze of lemon juice and salt to taste and leave to one side.

To make the bhajis, in a large bowl combine the cooked potato with all the remaining ingredients except the oil. Add 3–4 tablespoons of water to create a batter thick enough to bind the ingredients. Try not to break up the potato too much.

Fill a heavy-based pan one-third full with oil and heat to 180°C. If you don't have a thermometer, drop a little of the batter into the pan; if it sinks then rises, sizzling, your oil is hot enough. Using a dessertspoon, drop a spoonful of the bhaji mixture into the oil. It will bubble and come to the surface. You need to do this in batches so the oil temperature does not drop. Fry for about 5 minutes, ensuring that all sides of the bhajis turn a lovely golden colour. Once cooked, place on a plate covered in kitchen towel to drain.

To serve, put the purée into the middle of a big plate or platter. Balance the bhajis on the top and sprinkle with sliced spring onion and a little chilli.

vegetarian hassle free, **gluten free**

Carrot, Parsnip and Coriander Rostis

makes about
8 rostis

Rostis are a lovely way to change a well-loved, sometimes predictable vegetable into something special. These rostis are great served as a brunch dish with an egg.

1 tablespoon cumin seeds
1 tablespoon coriander seeds
250g carrot, grated
250g parsnip, grated
1 teaspoon sea salt
good grind of black pepper
20g fresh coriander, chopped
2 tablespoons cornflour
2 large eggs
sunflower oil, for frying
knob of unsalted butter

Toast the cumin and coriander seeds gently in a frying pan for a couple of minutes, until you can smell the spices and they start to pop; agitate the pan while frying to stop the seeds burning, which will make the spices bitter. Remove from the heat and use a pestle and mortar to grind to a fine powder.

My Tip
This spice mix will make more than you need for this recipe, but use it in curries or sprinkled over roasted aubergines with a little olive oil and lemon juice.

Place the carrot, parsnip, 1 teaspoon of the coriander and cumin mix, salt, black pepper and fresh coriander into a large bowl and combine thoroughly. Sprinkle over the cornflour and mix together really well. Add the eggs and stir through.

Heat a little oil in a large non-stick frying pan. Take a heaped tablespoonful of the mixture, place it carefully into the frying pan and press down; tidy up the sides with a spoon, just pushing them into making a round. Repeat with as many spoonfuls as you can fit in your frying pan. They will be a bit raggedy and the outside bits will go lovely and crispy, but you want to make as even a circle as you can. Each rosti should be about 1–1.5cm deep.

Fry slowly for about 5 minutes – take your time, we need to get the vegetables cooked. When the rostis are a deep golden brown, turn them over, add the knob of butter to the pan and cook the second side for a little less time, about 3 minutes.

Once cooked, place on a kitchen towel, then repeat the process with the next spoonful of batter. Serve when the batter is used up and all the rostis are ready.

My Tip
You will probably have some bits fall off as you fry each batch – you need to clear these out of the pan before you start a new batch.

Potato Cakes **Stuffed** with **Chickpeas** and **Coriander**

serves 2–4

These potato cakes are packed full of flavour and great made the day before and kept in the fridge, ready to cook when you want them. You can serve as a main with a big salad or as a starter with one potato cake each.

For the filling
2 banana shallots, finely chopped
1 red chilli, finely chopped
3 tablespoons unsalted butter
75g fresh tomato, chopped
2 teaspoons garam masala
¼ teaspoon turmeric
1 x 400g can of chickpeas, drained
50g spinach, chopped
10g basil, chopped, stalks included
sea salt

For the potato cakes
450g cold mashed potato
  (no seasoning)
½ teaspoon sea salt
50g unsalted butter, melted
*½ teaspoon **gluten-free** baking*
  powder
*25g **gluten-free** plain flour*
  (plus extra for dusting)
¼ teaspoon xanthan gum
10g basil, finely chopped

For the herb sauce
100g fresh coriander, leaves picked
  and stalks discarded
100g fresh basil leaves
1 red chilli (seeds and pith removed
  if you don't like spice)
5 tablespoons natural yoghurt
lemon juice, to taste
sea salt, to taste

Preheat the oven to 200°C/180°C Fan/Gas Mark 6.

In a large frying pan, gently sauté the shallots and chilli in 1 tablespoon of the butter until tender and the onion is translucent. Add the tomato, garam masala, turmeric and salt to taste and cook for 3–5 minutes, until the tomato is easily broken down with a spoon into the pan.

Gently mash the tomatoes in the pan. Add the chickpeas and the remaining butter and turn the heat up a little to cook them through for a couple of minutes. Add in the chopped spinach and basil, turn off the heat and stir through until the spinach is wilted and cooked. Remove from the heat and leave to cool, then divide into four equal portions.

Put all of the potato cake ingredients into a large bowl and gently bring them together using your hands; don't over work the mixture. Divide them into four equal portions (about 110g each) and roll these into balls.

Lightly flour your work surface and hands. Take one of the potato balls and place it onto the floured surface. Gently press down and, using the outside of your hands, shape the potato ball into a flat circle approximately 13cm in diameter.

Place one portion of the filling mixture neatly into the middle, heaped high. Using a palette knife, bring the sides up around the filling mixture, ensuring there are no holes and the filling is evenly covered. Shape with your hands until you have a neat ball. Press down and continue shaping into a circular shape until you have a patty about 7.5cm round and 2.5cm high. Repeat the process with the remaining three portions.

Place in the oven for 10–12 minutes. Alternatively, fry for 3–4 minutes on each side until crispy and golden.

To make the herb sauce, finely chop the coriander, basil and chilli and combine with the yoghurt and lemon juice. Season with salt to taste and then drizzle over the potato cakes and serve.

Sweet Potato Pancakes – Savoury and Sweet

makes 16 pancakes

I make these at weekends as they are good for breakfast or brunch. I make one batch of sweet and one batch of savoury batter, and they last for the whole weekend for the family. The batter will keep when covered for up to four days, which is perfect as I know how difficult breakfast can be for people on a gluten-free diet. They are so quick to cook once you have made the batter.

Feel free to add in your own flavour combinations; just try to steer clear of ingredients that are too wet.

450g sweet potatoes, roasted in their skins
300g **gluten-free** plain flour
4 teaspoons **gluten-free** baking powder
1 teaspoon sea salt
3 large eggs
75g unsalted butter, melted
425ml milk
sunflower oil, for frying

For the savoury pancakes
○ 1 red chilli or ½ teaspoon sriracha
4–5 spring onions, finely chopped
20g coriander, chopped
1 teaspoon sea salt
juice of ½ lime

For the sweet pancakes
2 tablespoons caster sugar
100g blueberries or sultanas
1 teaspoon mixed spice
juice of 1 lemon

Peel the skin from the roasted sweet potatoes and put the flesh into a large bowl. Don't worry if some bits are darker than others; it just adds more flavour to the pancakes.

Add the flour, baking powder, salt, eggs and butter to the bowl and combine to a dough, then slowly whisk in the milk until you have a thick batter.

Now split the batter into two, and add the ingredients for the savoury version into one half, and the ingredients for the sweet version into the other half, combining well. (Alternatively, you can use the mixture during the course of the week to make batches for breakfast.)

Put a splash of sunflower oil in a good non-stick frying pan and drop a heaped tablespoon of the batter into the pan. Cook for about 2 minutes, until the batter is a dark golden colour and then, using a spatula, gently flip and cook the other side until that too is dark and golden.

When flipped you will see from the side of the pancake if cooked all the way through. If it looks wet you need to continue cooking; if it's springy and dry it's done. Remove from the pan and reserve until you have finished cooking all the pancakes.

My Tips
If you have a waffle iron, this mixture works brilliantly in that.

The savoury pancakes are lovely served with fried eggs and avocado. You can make these a bit more substantial if you add in some sweetcorn; canned is fine. The sweet pancakes are delicious when covered in cream and maple syrup.

Stuffed Beefsteak Tomatoes
with **Butterbeans** and
Mediterranean Vegetables

serves 4

For me there is something so evocative about stuffed tomatoes. They were very much a staple of the 1970s dinner party and as such, I think, have fallen a bit out of fashion but when done well, wow, they are wonderful. This is one of my very favourite ways to serve them, stuffed with a simple vegetable and butterbean stew.

4 firm beefsteak tomatoes (I use a mix of heritage varieties)
3–4 tablespoons olive oil, plus extra for drizzling
1 medium aubergine, chopped into small chunks
1 courgette, chopped into small chunks
1 tablespoon fresh oregano leaves, picked, or 1 teaspoon dried
3 garlic cloves, minced
good pinch of black pepper
225g drained butterbeans (I use large ones from a jar but canned is fine)
1 tablespoon balsamic vinegar
10g chopped chives, plus some for serving
sea salt

Preheat the oven to 200°C/180°C Fan/Gas Mark 6. Cut the tops off the tomatoes, leaving the stalk on and enough of a top for it to act like a hat on the tomato. Gently remove and reserve the pulp and pips but leave the tomato whole.

Place the olive oil into a pan with the aubergine and a good pinch of salt and gently fry off for approximately 3–5 minutes, until the aubergine is slightly cooked and has absorbed the oil; you will need to stir occasionally but resist the temptation to add more oil.

Add the courgette, oregano, tomato pulp, garlic and black pepper to the pan and fry until the aubergine is cooked, about 5 minutes. Remove from the heat. Add the butterbeans, balsamic vinegar and chopped chives and combine. Taste and adjust the seasoning if necessary.

Gently spoon the mixture into the empty tomatoes, pressing it down carefully to preserve the shape of the fruit and overfilling the tomatoes slightly. Put the tomatoes on a lightly oiled roasting tin and put the tops on (it doesn't have to be perfect), then drizzle lightly with olive oil.

Place in the oven and cook for 20–25 minutes. You want the tomatoes just cooked so they retain their shape.

These are best served warm, drizzled with a little more olive oil and sprinkled liberally with chopped chives. I love to serve them with a big frittata, try the Spaghetti Frittata (page 28), or Spanish omelette and a balsamic dressed green salad.

My tip
When I took part in MasterChef, *someone mentioned a tomato knife and I had no idea what they were talking about. They are very cheap but when chopping tomatoes they totally make the difference. Beware – they can also chop your fingers!*

Twice-cooked Cheese Soufflés

makes 8 soufflés

I am particularly proud of these soufflés. They make beautiful starter or brunch dishes and can be frozen or made a couple of days in advance to reheat on the day. I know soufflés are supposed to be tricky but if you follow the recipe, I promise you will have lovely results.

I use my muffin tin as I can rarely find eight ramekins!

For the tin
unsalted butter, for greasing
100–150g grated vegetarian Italian hard cheese (the cheap ready-grated cheese is perfect)

For the soufflés
75g milk
75g double cream
25g unsalted butter
30g cornflour
125g strong Cheddar cheese, grated
1 large egg, whole
1 large egg, separated

For the soufflé sauce
200ml double cream
50g vegetarian Italian hard cheese, grated

You will need
non-stick 12-hole muffin tin

Preheat the oven to 180°C/160°C Fan/Gas Mark 4. Liberally butter eight of the muffin holes and coat them with the grated vegetarian hard cheese.

Combine the milk and cream in a jug or bowl. Gently melt the butter over a low heat and add in the cornflour, beating with a wooden spoon, to form a roux. This will be shiny and in a lump. Gradually, and still over a low heat, add in the milk and cream mixture, beating all the time, ensuring there are no flour lumps. This will make a very thick sauce.

Add the grated cheese and whisk in quickly, using an electric whisk. You want the cheese to melt; don't worry if the sauce is a bit split and oily. Put to one side and leave to cool slightly for about 5 minutes.

Put the egg and egg yolk into a bowl and whisk lightly to combine. Slowly add the egg mixture to the sauce, whisking all the time.

Whisk the egg white until it forms stiff peaks. Using a spatula, put a large spoonful of the egg white into the cheese sauce mix, and gently combine, using a figure-of-eight motion, until all incorporated. Repeat until you have combined all of the egg white into the cheese sauce.

Put a large spoonful of the mixture in each of the buttered muffin tin holes and place in the oven for 18–20 minutes, until fluffed up and golden.

My Tip
You can freeze the soufflés at this stage or put them into the fridge for up to 48 hours before continuing as below.

Place the soufflés on a baking tray. Pour over the double cream and grate over the vegetarian Italian hard cheese. Return to the oven for 10–15 minutes, until the soufflés are nicely glazed and risen and the cream is thickened. I serve straight away, on a bed of lightly dressed watercress sitting on a spoonful of the thickened cheesy cream from the baking tray.

Blue Cheese Soufflés with Caramelised Pear and Walnut Salad

makes 12 soufflés

This recipe follows exactly the same steps as the recipe for Twice-cooked Cheese Soufflés (page 40), but adds a little something special. If you love blue cheese you will love these. The pear salad can be prepared earlier on the same day as the soufflés, or even the day before if you don't mind having the pears cold.

For the soufflés
see page 40, but replace the Cheddar with 125g crumbled Stilton or other blue cheese

For the pear and walnut salad
2–3 ripe Conference pears
splash of sunflower oil
50g unsalted butter
1 tablespoon sugar
50g walnuts, roughly chopped
½ teaspoon cracked black pepper
3 tablespoons olive oil
2 tablespoons white wine vinegar
1 pack of mixed dark green leaves
(rocket, spinach, watercress)
½ red onion, finely sliced
sea salt

Make the blue cheese soufflés according to the recipe on page 40 but add 125g crumbled Stilton or your favourite blue instead of Cheddar.

To make the pear and walnut salad, cut the pears in half and remove the core with a melon baller or teaspoon. Then slice them lengthways into segments. The base of each segment should be about 1.5cm. You want about three segments per soufflé portion.

Put the splash of sunflower oil into a saucepan and gently melt the butter. Place the pears in the pan flesh-side down and sprinkle with the sugar. Cook until just golden, then flip over and repeat. Remove and reserve.

Immediately put the walnuts into the pan with the black pepper and toss through. Keep stirring until golden, about 1 minute, then remove and reserve on a greaseproof paper-covered plate.

To assemble the salad, combine the olive oil and white wine vinegar in a bowl and drizzle over the salad leaves until just coated. Add a little salt to taste.

Place the salad leaves on plates and sprinkle over the walnuts and a little finely sliced red onion. Place three slices of caramelised pear to one side and on the other side place the heated blue cheese soufflé with a little of the cream sauce from the bottom of the baking tray. Serve immediately.

My Tip
Use one of the drier Stilton-type cheeses. The really creamy ones can be a little fatty for this dish and the soufflés don't work quite as well. If you want more of the blue cheese hit you could add a little blue cheese instead of vegetarian Italian hard cheese into the cream sauce when reheating, but I found this to be really strong.

Gypsy Potatoes

serves 4 as
a side

This dish is very loosely based on one of my favourite tapas dishes but that is covered in truffles. If you happen to have some around then please feel free to grate generously all over; otherwise, however, just serve this dish as is. It's a wonderful dish, very rich and indulgent, and when served with asparagus in particular it's superb as part of a big veggie feast. You don't need to drain the potatoes; we want to use the starch to give us a lovely sauce.

100g unsalted butter
6 shallots, finely chopped
8 sprigs of fresh thyme, leaves picked
2 sage leaves, finely chopped
4 garlic cloves
500g potatoes (King Edwards or Red Roosters), grated
○ *750ml vegetable stock*
4 large eggs, separated , optional
sea salt, to taste

My Tip
Work quickly once the potatoes are grated as they go brown very quickly.

Preheat the oven to 180°C/160°C Fan/Gas Mark 4. I like to use a pan that can go on the stove top and then into the oven for this dish but if you don't have one then you can transfer into an oven dish.

Heat the butter gently in a pan, then add the shallots, thyme, sage and garlic. Gently fry for 4–5 minutes, until really soft but not coloured.

Add the grated potato and stir to combine all the ingredients well. Add the stock and stir again; season with a little salt (depending on the saltiness of your stock) and place in the oven for about 20–25 minutes, until the potato has soaked up nearly all the stock.

I like to make this dish extra special and indulgent and add an egg yolk for each guest. To do this, remove the potatoes from the oven and make four wells in the potato mixture using the back of a tablespoon. Gently place one egg yolk in each of the wells and return to the oven for about 4 minutes, until the egg is cooked but still lovely and runny.

Remove from the oven and serve.

My Tip
If using egg yolks, freeze the egg whites to use in meringues or to thicken soups – you can do this in ice trays for ease of use.

Sweet and Salty Ras El Hanout Popcorn

serves 4

Popcorn is a favourite snack; it's so very easy and versatile to dress up to something a bit special. This is great for when watching a movie, but I also put it out for guests to snack on before I dish up dinner.

2 tablespoons sunflower oil
100g popping corn kernels
3 teaspoons sea salt flakes
2 teaspoons granulated sugar
1 teaspoon Ras El Hanout
* spice mix*

You will need
large tight-lidded saucepan

Place the oil in a large saucepan with the popcorn kernels. Put the lid on the pan and turn the heat up. Keep the lid on tightly and wait for the popcorn to start popping.

Gently agitate the saucepan as the corn pops and listen for when it stops or nearly stops popping. Remove from the heat.

Mix the sea salt flakes, sugar and Ras El Hanout in a separate bowl and sprinkle over the popped corn while it's still hot, stirring to coat as much of it as you can.

Serve within a few hours of making.

My Tip
Experiment with flavours and spices. Smoked paprika and garam masala work well too.

vegetarian hassle free, **gluten free**

Goat's Cheese and Watercress Pie with Walnuts

serves 6

One of my favourite dishes is the herb pie served in the Mediterranean. For years it was my go-to vegetarian dish, but this is my very English take on it using some of my best-loved Hampshire ingredients.

unsalted butter, for greasing
1 large onion, chopped
splash of olive oil
200g celery, finely chopped
50g spring onion, chopped
2 large eggs
400g watercress, chopped, stalks included, plus extra for garnish
50g mustard and cress, chopped
5g fresh thyme, leaves picked
zest and juice of 1 lemon
100g walnuts, roughly chopped
100g strong Cheddar cheese, grated
100g ricotta cheese
250g mild creamy goat's cheese
good grind of black pepper
*350–400g Rough Puff and Flaky Pastry (page 196) or 1 pack of **gluten-free** ready made*
1 large egg, beaten, to egg wash

You will need
20cm square pie dish

Preheat the oven to 200°C/180°C Fan/Gas Mark 6. Grease the pie dish with butter.

Cook off the onion in a splash of olive oil until softened. Add half the celery and the spring onion and cook until wilted. Leave to cool.

Add the eggs, watercress, mustard and cress, thyme, lemon zest, chopped walnuts and remaining celery to the mixture with the cheeses. Season with lemon juice and black pepper to taste.

Place the mixture in the pie dish and leave to cool. Cover with the pastry, egg wash well and cut a small cross in the top of the pastry.

Bake in the oven for 20–25 minutes, until the pastry is crispy and golden. I like to serve this pie warm with some roast tomatoes.

My Tip
You can mix this up using different cheeses and herbs to add your own spin to this lovely vegetarian dish.

Pizza Tart

serves 4–6

Some flavours are so very classically simple that I nearly didn't include this recipe in the book; however it's such a beautiful thing to eat that I got outvoted by the rest of the house. I'm so glad I did include it; it's something I cook all the time in the summer, and we love it.

*1 x quantity Shortcrust Pastry (page 198) or 1 pack of **gluten-free** ready-made (there is less pastry in the ready-made roll)*
100g crème fraîche
125g strong Cheddar cheese
50g mascarpone cheese
20g basil, finely chopped, stalks included, plus a few small leaves to decorate the top
150g cherry tomatoes, cut into quarters
sea salt and black pepper

You will need
small 25 x 17cm roasting tray
baking beans

Preheat the oven to 200°C/180°C Fan/Gas Mark 6.

Roll out the pastry to the thickness of a £1 coin, making it about 1cm wider than your tin. Gently lay the pastry over the tin, and press it into the corners using your fingers. Generously line the pastry with a sheet of greaseproof paper so it comes up past the top of the tin by about 2cm all round. (If using shop-bought pastry you can often use the paper it came wrapped in.)

Pour in your baking beans and cook for about 15–20 minutes, until the pastry is firm and lightly golden. You can tell if the pastry is ready by removing the tart from the oven and just carefully pulling back the greaseproof; if the pastry is waxy and soft it needs a little more cooking.

Once cooked, remove the beans and greaseproof. You may need to trim the edges or tidy up any excess pastry with a small knife.

Combine the crème fraîche, Cheddar, mascarpone and basil in a bowl with a pinch of sea salt and a good grind of black pepper.

Place the crème fraîche mixture over the bottom of the tart and scatter over the chopped tomatoes and some basil leaves.

Bake the tart for 15 minutes, until set and just starting to turn golden. For best results serve warm.

vegetarian hassle free, **gluten free**

The Best Extra Cheesy Extra Garlicky Bread

serves 4

This is my ultimate treat and works beautifully with pasta dishes. It really is the very best to snack on when you want the most satisfying comfort food in front of the TV on a Friday night.

*1 x 25–30cm **gluten-free** baguette, French stick or French Bread (page 183), cut in half*
25g unsalted butter
5–6 garlic cloves (adjust for your taste), finely chopped
175g mozzarella cheese, grated
25g strong Cheddar cheese, grated
5g flat-leaf parsley, finely chopped

Either preheat the grill or preheat the oven to 220°C/200°C Fan/Gas Mark 7. Lightly toast the gluten-free baguette or French stick.

Very gently, over the lowest heat, melt the butter and garlic together for a minute or two. Do not brown, just release as much of the garlic flavour as you can and cook it through so that the garlic is soft.

Remove from the heat and add in the mozzarella, Cheddar and parsley. Stir together thoroughly; it may melt a little, but it will be fine.

Spoon evenly over the lightly toasted bread and place in the oven or under the grill until golden and bubbling and meltingly good.

Serve when the cheese is not too hot to burn your mouth.

My Tip
I often find it quicker and easier to use my scissors to finely cut herbs like tarragon, parsley or coriander.

vegetarian hassle free, **gluten free**

Asian-style Mushroom and Vegetable Broth

serves 2 as
a main or 4
for lunch

I love spicy Asian-style soups and this broth base is a real favourite. You can make it a few days in advance and keep it in the fridge or freeze it in portions so that you can put something together quickly when you are really pushed for time. Don't be put off by the long list of ingredients; it's very simple to make and you can serve it with whatever veg you wish. I've included some of my favourites to give you a pointer.

For the broth
40g dried mixed mushrooms
1 litre boiling water
splash of sunflower oil
1 onion, diced
1 red chilli, finely sliced
1 stalk of lemongrass, well bruised
½ tablespoon grated fresh ginger
3 garlic cloves, chopped
1 sheet nori (optional)
*60ml **gluten-free** soy sauce*
2 tablespoons rice wine vinegar

To make the soup
200g mixed or button mushrooms, chopped
110g asparagus, chopped
1 bok choi, green leaves chopped off, base chopped into 4 or 8 depending on size
1 red pepper, finely sliced
75g beansprouts

To serve
75g cooked rice per person
2–3 spring onions, finely sliced, green parts included
5g coriander, chopped
5g basil, chopped
a little red chilli, finely chopped
10g (approx.) unsalted peanuts, roughly chopped (optional)

Place the dried mushrooms in a bowl with the boiling water and leave for at least 20 minutes until stewed, or overnight.

Heat the oil in a large saucepan and gently fry off the onion and chilli until cooked through and softened, about 3 minutes. Add in the lemongrass, ginger and garlic and cook for a further 1 minute.

My Tip
I always cook the onions, then add in the garlic for just a minute or two before adding more ingredients. Onions take longer to cook than garlic and burnt garlic is very bitter and can really spoil your dish before you start.

Put the soaked dried mushrooms and stock into the pan with the nori (if using; this adds a fishy flavour to the broth in much the same way fish sauce would, so leave out if you prefer), soy sauce and rice wine vinegar. Bring to the boil and simmer for 5 minutes.

Remove from the heat, strain and reserve the stock, discarding the vegetables. Use immediately; or cool and keep in the fridge for 48 hours in a covered dish or freeze.

To make the soup, bring the stock to the boil and add all the ingredients except the beansprouts. Leave to boil for up to 1 minute, turn off the heat and add in the beansprouts. Stir through and serve immediately.

To serve, divide the rice among your serving bowls, spoon over the broth with the vegetables, and sprinkle on the spring onions, herbs, chilli and peanuts, if using.

My Tip
Rice noodles work really well in this dish as well; just cook according to the packet instructions and add them to the broth instead of the rice.

Chestnut and Mushroom Soup

serves 4–6

I love chestnuts, particularly now that you can buy them vacuum packed. They add an earthy warmth to dishes and in autumn/winter I often use them in dishes to add an extra depth of flavour. This simple soup is wonderful and so easy to do. It's great to serve as a starter or a lunch-time dish with crusty bread.

50g unsalted butter
splash of sunflower oil
1 onion, chopped
2–3 garlic cloves, chopped
3 fresh sage leaves, chopped
6 sprigs of fresh thyme, picked
180g vacuum-packed chestnuts
450g white mushrooms,
* roughly chopped*
750ml vegetable stock
sea salt and black pepper

To serve (optional)
*crusty **gluten-free** bread*
mushrooms and chestnuts, finely
* sliced and fried*
fresh thyme leaves

Place the butter, oil, onion, garlic, sage and thyme in a large saucepan and gently sauté for about 3 minutes, until the onions and garlic are softened and clear.

My Tip
When using fresh thyme hold the stalk at the top and gently run your fingers down the stalk, going against the way the leaves are growing. The small leaves will just fall straight into the pan; it's so much easier than picking individual leaves. If the thyme is young the stalks will be softer so you may just be able to chop finely.

Add the chestnuts and mushrooms and cook gently for a further 7–8 minutes, until the mushrooms are cooked through and juicy.

Place in a liquidiser or food processor with the vegetable stock and blitz until smooth. Add salt and black pepper to taste – I do this at the end because it will depend on the saltiness of your stock.

Serve hot in bowls with crusty gluten-free bread. I like to sprinkle some fried mushroom and chestnuts on the top of the soup bowls, with a little fresh thyme to add some texture as well.

Cauliflower and Tarragon Soup

serves 4–6

Sometimes the easiest of things are the most delicious. This soup could not be simpler but is delicious, especially if you have a cauliflower that is a little wilted and needs using. It's great to make a quick soup that can be frozen for another day if needed.

1 medium-sized cauliflower, cut into small pieces
1 vegetable stock cube
7g tarragon
sea salt and black pepper

For the tarragon oil, to finish (optional)
100ml rapeseed oil
7g tarragon, finely chopped

Put the cauliflower, vegetable stock cube and tarragon into a saucepan and cover with water until just submerged. Bring to the boil and simmer until tender. Drain and pick out the smaller pieces of cauliflower for garnish; reserve the stock.

Using a stick blender or liquidiser, blend the cauliflower until creamy, adding some of the reserved stock until you get the consistency of soup you like. (The current trend is for very thick soups but I prefer mine a little runnier.) Season with salt and pepper to taste.

To make the tarragon oil, put the oil and tarragon stalks in a saucepan and fry very gently over the lowest possible heat for at least 20 minutes. If you bash the tarragon stalks with a wooden spoon it releases more oils and flavour. After 20 minutes remove the oil from the heat, drain through a sieve and reserve. Crumble the leaves from the tarragon stalks; reserve the leaves for garnish and replace the stalks in the oil (they will add flavour).

To serve, sprinkle some of the reserved pieces of cauliflower over the top of the soup, swirl with the tarragon oil and sprinkle over some of the crispy tarragon leaves from the oil. Garnish with a good grind of black pepper and serve.

My Tip
If you don't want to make the tarragon oil and fried tarragon you can dress this simply with the cauliflower pieces, a little cream or olive oil and a good grind of black pepper. If you like a richer soup you may want to add some double cream to the soup as well.

................................main event

Three-cheese and Mushroom Lasagne

serves 4–6

I love this recipe – it's the one where I definitely get my carnivore friends eating a vegetarian dish and not commenting that they feel they have missed out on something. It's also easy to prepare. We serve it with big bowls of salad and The Best Extra Cheesy Extra Garlicky Bread (page 48) so it's definitely a sharing dish that's lovely to bring to the table for people to help themselves.

approx. 8 **gluten-free** lasagne sheets

For the base
400g big flat mushrooms, roughly chopped
400g white mushrooms, roughly chopped
50g flat-leaf parsley, stalks included, chopped
10g thyme leaves
4 garlic cloves, thinly sliced or chopped
100g unsalted butter
175g garlic and herb cream cheese
sea salt and black pepper, to taste

For the white cheese sauce
40g cornflour
400ml milk, plus extra to make a paste
250g halloumi cheese, grated
150g Cheddar cheese, grated
sea salt and black pepper

Alternatively, if you are vegan, use the recipe for Vegan Cheese Sauce on page 210, and double the quantities

You will need
25 x 8cm lasagne dish or similar

Preheat the oven to 180°C/160°C Fan/Gas Mark 4.

Place in a large saucepan with all the ingredients for the base except the cream cheese. Gently sauté until the mushrooms are cooked and juicy. Stir in the cream cheese and put to one side.

Make the cheese sauce by mixing the cornflour with a little milk until you have a paste the consistency of double cream. Bring the 400ml milk to the boil and pour into the cornflour mixture, stirring or whisking all the time until you have a thick white sauce. Keep stirring for a further couple of minutes.

Turn off the heat and add the grated halloumi and most of the Cheddar, retaining a little for sprinkling on top of the lasagne. Season with black pepper and a little salt; but be careful; the cheese is already salty so don't add too much. Whisk until the sauce is smooth. If you have a little halloumi not melted don't worry; it will melt in the oven.

To assemble the lasagne, place half the cooked mushrooms and liquid into the dish, cover with a sheet of lasagne and pour over half the sauce. Repeat with the rest of the mushrooms, lasagne sheets and sauce, then sprinkle on the last bits of Cheddar and place in the oven for around 25–30 minutes, until the top is golden and bubbling and the lasagne is cooked through. Remove and leave to rest for 5 minutes before serving.

My Tip
A lot of traditionally made cheese uses rennet and is not vegetarian. There are many major brands that are suitable, but you do need to check before buying.

Sweet Potato and Bean 'Meatballs' with **Basil** and Tomato Sauce

serves 3–4

This is a bit of a cheat meal in that I use one of my store cupboard favourites – red kidney beans in chilli sauce. But I am a huge believer in cheats if you can still end up with a lovely meal. These are surprisingly light and I find that roasting them is healthier and gives a much better result than frying meatballs.

For the 'meatballs'
splash of sunflower oil
1 red onion, finely chopped
1 red chilli, finely chopped
1 garlic clove, finely chopped or grated
○ *1 x 400g can of red kidney beans in chilli sauce, drained and sauce reserved*
250g sweet potato mash from a roasted jacket sweet potato
10g basil, chopped, stalks included
sea salt

For the tomato sauce
1 x 400g can chopped tomatoes
○ *sauce from the can of kidney beans above*
5g basil, chopped, plus extra to decorate
sea salt

Preheat the oven to 180°C/160°C Fan/Gas Mark 4. Line a baking tray with greaseproof paper.

Heat the oil in a non-stick frying pan and gently fry off the onion and red chilli for 3–5 minutes, until translucent. Add in the garlic and cook for a further 2 minutes, stirring so the garlic does not burn. Leave to cool.

Put the drained kidney beans into a large bowl and mash; you want to break up the beans but leave some texture. Then add in the roasted sweet potato flesh, the chopped basil and the cooked onion/chilli mixture. Season with a pinch of sea salt and mash to combine.

Roll into balls about the size of a table tennis ball and place onto your baking tray.

Place in the oven for 40–45 minutes, turning halfway through, until the 'meatballs' are crispy on the outside and roasting to a golden colour.

About 10 minutes before serving, put the chopped tomatoes into a pan (I use the one I cooked the onion mixture in) with the sauce from the kidney beans and the basil. Simmer for about 5–7 minutes, until the sauce has thickened and reduced. Add in a pinch of salt to taste.

To serve, place the tomato sauce into the bottom of the bowl and place the 'meatballs' on top. You can finely slice some fresh basil to decorate if you want. I serve these with a big green salad and some gluten-free bread, but rice works well too.

My Tip
I often roast sweet potatoes in their jackets and will throw an extra one in to use in these 'meatballs' or other dishes. It's important to use the flesh from a sweet potato that's been roasted in its jacket, not boiled, as the boiled version will be too wet.

vegetarian hassle free, **gluten free**

Whole Roast Romanesco Cauliflower with Rich Onion Sauce

serves 2–4

I really love the idea of bringing a whole roast vegetable to the table and being able to carve it as one would a roast, making it a real centrepiece on the table. In this recipe I use a Romanesco cauliflower just to add to the interest of the dish, but an ordinary cauliflower works just as well.

For the cauliflower
1 whole Romanesco cauliflower
drizzle of flavourless oil
50g unsalted butter
sea salt and black pepper

For the onion sauce
50g unsalted butter
3 onions, chopped
3–4 garlic cloves, peeled and
  left whole
200ml double cream
sea salt and black pepper, to taste

You will need
deep-lidded roasting dish or a dish
  that can be sealed with tin foil

Preheat the oven to 180°C/160°C Fan/Gas Mark 4.

Place the cauliflower into the roasting pot and drizzle with oil, knobs of butter and a good grind of sea salt and pepper. Put the lid or tin foil on and place in the oven for about 50 minutes, until tender when pierced with a skewer or sharp knife. Remove the lid, baste and turn up the oven to 200°C/180°C Fan/Gas Mark 6. Cook for a further 10 minutes, until the cauliflower turns a nice golden colour.

In the meantime, put the butter, onions, and garlic into a pan and sauté very slowly over the lowest possible heat for about 20–25 minutes; you want the onion to be soft and melting and you should be able to easily squash the garlic cloves to a pulp with the back of a spoon. The onions might colour a little to a golden brown, but you don't want them to be crispy or have a darker colour.

Add in the double cream. You can just mash the onion and cream at this stage or purée in a blender or through a sieve; it's up to you, they will taste great regardless. Season with salt and black pepper and reserve.

To serve, remove the whole cauliflower from the tin, place on a plate, pour over the sauce and take to the table.

My Tip
The onion sauce goes wonderfully with most fish and meats. I use it with many dishes to add an extra dimension of flavour and texture, particularly puréed. You can of course just boil the cauliflower florets for ease and make the sauce, if you prefer.

vegetarian hassle free, **gluten free**

Sweet and Sour
Crispy Tempeh

serves 2–4

I must admit that since Rebecca went vegetarian, I've had to really stretch my knowledge and re-educate myself in so many ways. This dish is based on my quick sweet and sour sauce with crispy chicken. It uses tempeh, which is a traditional high-protein soy product with more texture than tofu, and I think it works very well in this dish. I order mine in jars online so it's to hand whenever I need it. This dish is lovely served with plain or egg fried rice.

*50ml **gluten-free** soy sauce*
50g cornflour
1 x 400g jar of tempeh, drained
  and chopped into bite-sized pieces
sunflower oil, for frying
1 x quantity of Sweet and Sour
  Sauce (page 205)
½ mild red chilli, deseeded and
  finely chopped, to serve
sprinkling of chopped onions,
  to serve

Combine the soy sauce and cornflour with 50ml water in a shallow bowl and place the chopped tempeh into it to marinate. Leave for at least 20 minutes.

Fill a heavy-based pan one-third full with oil and heat to a temperature of 180°C. If you don't have a thermometer, simply drop a little of the tempeh into the pan; if it sinks then rises, sizzling, your oil is hot enough. Alternatively, use a deep fat fryer.

Add the tempeh to the hot oil, being careful not to splash, and stir so that it's completely covered. Leave to cook until it's a deep golden brown, about 4 minutes. Remove and drain onto kitchen towel.

Add the crispy tempeh to the sweet and sour sauce, and stir so that the tempeh is coated with the sauce. Serve immediately in bowls with plain white rice and a sprinkle of fresh chilli and chopped onion over the top.

Open-topped
Deep Pizza Pie

serves 4–6

If you are like me and think the topping is by far the best part of the pizza, then this is the recipe for you. It's great served warm but can be used cold for buffets and picnics. I have also made these in muffin tins for individual pies. I've suggested using my foolproof shortcrust pastry, but a ready-made pastry can be bought if you are in a rush.

For the case
1 x quantity Shortcrust Pastry (page 198), or shop-bought **gluten-free** pastry
1 large egg, beaten, to egg wash

For the pizza sauce
1 x 500g carton of tomato passata
2–3 tablespoons dried herbs
1/2 teaspoon sugar
1 tablespoon olive oil

For the filling
400g large tomatoes, beef or similar
pinch of sea salt
1 medium red onion, chopped
splash of olive oil
2 garlic cloves, minced
2 large flat mushrooms, roughly chopped
1 small courgette, thinly sliced
25g basil, roughly chopped, plus extra for sprinkling
1 red pepper, chopped
handful of pitted olives (optional)
250g mozzarella and 150g strong Cheddar, grated and mixed together
dried mixed herbs for sprinkling

You will need
20cm springform tin
baking beans

Preheat the oven to 200°C/180°C Fan/Gas Mark 6. Line your tin with the pastry and blind bake for approximately 12 minutes (see page 46).

Slice the tomatoes to the depth of a £1 coin and place on a tray lined with kitchen towel. Sprinkle over a pinch of salt and then cover with kitchen towel to take out a little extra moisture.

Place all the ingredients for the pizza sauce in a pan and cook over a medium heat. Be careful – this has a tendency to spit. Reduce until about half remains and the sauce is thick and glossy.

Add the onion and a splash of olive oil to a saucepan and sauté until translucent in colour, about 2–3 minutes. Add the garlic, mushrooms and courgette and cook for a further 3–4 minutes, until cooked through. Remove from the heat and stir through the basil, red pepper and olives, if using. Allow to cool.

To assemble, place half the reduced pizza sauce over the bottom of the pie case. Cover with half the cooked vegetables, followed by a layer of the sliced tomatoes, and then half the mozzarella and Cheddar mix.

Repeat the process, sprinkling in a little chopped basil or some dried mixed herbs along with the final layer of cheese. Place in the oven for 20 minutes, until the top is golden and bubbling. Remove and leave to cool for 15 minutes, then serve. Perfect for lunch or with a large green salad for dinner.

My Tip
Feel free to change the ingredients, though I would suggest staying away from anything too wet as it will affect the structure of the pie. Use the ready-shredded pizza mozzarella, not the expensive stuff which is far too wet for this recipe. I have substituted vegan cheese with good results.

Roasted Broccoli with **Romesco Sauce** and **Roast Garlic Tahini**

64

serves 4

I am very lucky as Ben will eat broccoli and carrots raw as a snack as soon as he enters the house. This is also a favourite of Sam's, so much so he asked for the recipe to make it for his girlfriend! The colours are really beautiful on the plate and it tastes delicious.

For the broccoli
1 large broccoli
sunflower oil
1 small bulb of garlic
sea salt and black pepper

For the romesco sauce
125g blanched almonds
225g roasted red peppers from a jar, plus 2 tablespoons brine from the jar
1 tablespoon lemon juice
½ teaspoon smoked paprika
50ml extra virgin olive oil
1 teaspoon sea salt

For the tahini dressing
1½ tablespoons tahini
2–3 tablespoons extra virgin olive oil
½–1 tablespoon lemon juice
pinch sea salt

To serve (optional)
toasted flaked almonds
drizzle of Chilli Oil (page 212)

Preheat the oven to 180°C/160°C Fan/Gas Mark 4.

Cut the broccoli into steaks about 1.5cm thick; don't waste any florets that fall off, place them on an oiled baking tray with the broccoli steaks. Lightly coat the broccoli with a little oil and season with sea salt and black pepper. Cut the garlic bulb in half horizontally and place cut-side down on the baking tray. Transfer to the oven and roast for about 20 minutes, turning once halfway through. You want the broccoli to be tender and golden brown on the outside.

While the broccoli is roasting, make the romesco sauce. Place all the ingredients into a blender and pulse. I like to keep this with some texture in it, so you want a mixture slightly coarser than hummus; chunks of almond are fine.

My tip
If you don't have a food processor, use ground almonds and very finely chop the red pepper, and combine with the rest of the ingredients.

To make the tahini dressing, squeeze half of the garlic from the roasted garlic into a pestle and mortar and add the tahini. Combine well until it forms a smooth paste and add the olive oil, lemon juice and salt to make a smooth sauce. If you like lots of garlic add more from the roasted bulb.

To serve, place the romesco sauce on the bottom of a plate, arrange the broccoli, including any little crispy bits, over the top and drizzle with the tahini dressing. I like to dress this with lightly toasted flaked almonds and a drizzle of the chilli oil.

My Tips
Don't be put off by the different processes, they are very straightforward. The sauce and tahini dressing can be made the day before and kept in the fridge. Any leftover roasted garlic will keep in the fridge and is great to add to dressings or sauces.

vegetarian hassle free, **gluten free**

Warm Harissa-spiced Butternut Squash, Chickpeas and **Spinach Salad**

serves 6–8

I think a salad should not just be for summer but something you can enjoy the whole year round. This one is full of lovely warming flavours and ingredients so perfect for autumn and winter. It works wonderfully well with poached eggs for a simple supper or brunch.

1 butternut squash, cut into
  2.5cm cubes
2 red onions, cut into chunks
2 tablespoons harissa paste
1 tablespoon lemon juice
good pinch of sea salt
splash of sunflower oil
2 x 400g cans of chickpeas, drained
  (approx. 480g drained weight)
1 x 240g pack baby leaf spinach
50g toasted pine nuts, to serve

Preheat the oven to 180°C/160°C Fan/Gas Mark 4.

Combine the squash, onions, harissa, lemon juice and salt on a roasting tray and toss in the oil. Place in the oven for 20 minutes.

Remove from the oven, stir through the chickpeas and return to the oven for a further 10 minutes.

Remove and stir through the spinach until wilted. Sprinkle over the toasted pine nuts and serve.

You might want to add a little extra lemon juice and salt, but taste to see.

My Tip
The reserved chickpea water makes wonderful meringues. Try the Aquafaba (Vegan Meringue) Chocolate Mousse (page 144) or the Layered Pavlova with Pears, Chocolate and Chestnut (page 157).

vegetarian hassle free, **gluten free**

Puy Lentil, Pomegranate, Spinach and Feta Salad with Walnut

serves 6–8

Puy lentils are a real favourite of mine and I think they work particularly well with this salad. It's one of those dishes often found on my buffet-style lunches as it's so easy and goes a long way.

200g puy lentils
1 x 125g bag baby spinach
1 x 200g pack feta cheese, chopped
  into 1cm cubes
200g pomegranate seeds
50g walnuts, roughly chopped
25g chopped flat-leaf parsley
25g torn basil leaves

For the dressing
3 tablespoons sherry vinegar
3 tablespoons pomegranate molasses
6 tablespoons olive oil

Place the puy lentils in a saucepan with 600ml water and bring to the boil. Simmer for 20–25 minutes, until the lentils are cooked but firm to the bite.

Once the lentils are cooked, drain and rinse under boiling water. Return to the saucepan and mix in the spinach to wilt. Leave to cool.

Mix the dressing ingredients together and add to the lentil mixture, mixing well but without breaking the lentils down.

Add the chopped feta, pomegranate seeds, walnuts, parsley and basil (saving a little for serving), and mix in. Sprinkle the remainder on the top and serve.

Charred Vegetable Salsa, Roast Tomatoes and Halloumi

serves 4–6

This can make a beautiful dish on its own served with the lovely crusty gluten-free French Bread on page 183 or else as part of a spread of food – the colours just sing of summer. I have also prepared it indoors on a grill pan for those wonderful English summer rainy days. Don't be scared to really char the veg.

69

150g heritage tomatoes (you can use red if you prefer)
1 garlic bulb
1 large red pepper, whole
1 red onion, cut into rings about 1.5cm thick, kept unseparated
1 long red chilli
15g basil, stalks included, small leaves picked off and saved
2 tablespoons extra-virgin olive oil
1 x 225g pack halloumi cheese
squeeze of lemon (optional)
sea salt (optional)

You will need
bbq or grill pan

If using heritage tomatoes, cut the bigger ones into quarters and leave the cherry ones whole.

Barbecue or use a grill pan to roast the tomatoes, garlic, pepper, onion and chilli until they are blackened and charred. Leave the garlic whole; this recipe only needs a couple of cloves but the roasted garlic can be used in many other dishes and kept wrapped in tin foil in the fridge once cooled.

My tip
I learnt this technique when I was in Mexico with MasterChef working with Enrique Olvera at Pujol. It's one of the top restaurants in the world, so you listen when he shows you how to do something. If I can take just a little of his magic and put it into my dishes, it makes me so very happy.

Once everything is blackened remove from the heat and cut the pepper in half lengthways. Using a spoon, remove the pith and seeds. For a milder sauce, remove the pith and seeds from the chilli too. If you like it spicy, just cut off the top green stem.

Place the pepper, onion, chilli and basil with two garlic cloves from the bulb into a food processor with 1 tablespoon of olive oil and blitz (just one quick blitz is sufficient). Alternatively, finely dice them.

Chop the halloumi into chunks and fry off in a frying pan with the remaining oil until golden and crispy.

To serve, put the charred vegetable salsa on a plate. Place the halloumi on top and spoon over the roasted tomatoes. Sprinkle with the baby basil leaves.

I don't add salt to this dish as I think the halloumi is salty enough and I wanted the vegetables to have a purity of flavour. However, please feel free to add salt and a spritz of lemon if you feel it needs it.

main event

Veggie Sunday Lunch

serves 4–6

I wanted to include recipes that you could bring to the table in the same way you would bring a big joint or fish; and this recipe for hasselback butternut squash certainly fits that bill and is perfect with all the trimmings for a delicious veggie roast.

The pea purée adds a splash of vibrant colour and a fabulous fresh flavour, while the citrussy sumac sprouts are a crowd pleaser.

sunflower oil
Gravy (page 211)
sea salt and black pepper

For the roast potatoes
450g King Edward (or similar) potatoes, cut up for roasting; I like to make them slightly smaller than regular roasties

For the hasselback butternut squash
1 butternut squash
1 garlic bulb, halved
6–8 fresh sage leaves
1 tablespoon smoked Chilli Oil (page 212)

For the Brussels sprouts
500g Brussels sprouts, trimmed and cut in half
2 teaspoons sumac

For the pea purée
300g frozen peas
3–4 tablespoons olive oil
squeeze of lemon juice

Preheat the oven to 180°C/160°C Fan/Gas Mark 4.

Bring a large saucepan of water to the boil and parboil the potatoes for 10–12 minutes; you should be able to pierce them easily with a sharp knife to about 0.5cm, with the insides still firm. Drain the potatoes and then gently toss them around so that the edges become fluffy. Place the potatoes in a baking tray with enough oil to coat them (this will depend on the size of your pan), sprinkle over 1 teaspoon of salt and turn the potatoes, ensuring all are evenly coated. Place in the oven for 1 hour, turning halfway through, until the potatoes are golden and crispy and delicious.

Meanwhile, prepare the butternut squash. Cut the butternut squash in half lengthways; scoop out the seeds and reserve. With the squash lying cut-side down, place a wooden spoon alongside one half of the squash. Use a large sharp knife to cut even slices into the squash about 0.5cm apart. Use your wooden spoon as a gauge to stop you cutting all the way through and to help make your cuts even in depth. Repeat with the second half of the squash.

Put one half of the garlic bulb into each half of the squash, tucking it into the hole left when you scraped the seeds out. Place the squash halves cut-side down onto a baking tray, putting half the sage leaves under each squash half. Drizzle over a little sunflower oil and the smoked chilli oil and sprinkle liberally with salt and black pepper. Place in the oven for about 1 hour until the squash is really tender when pierced with a sharp knife or cocktail stick.

Next, place the sprouts on a baking tray with just enough oil to coat them – don't have them sitting in a layer of oil as they get greasy quite easily. Sprinkle over the sumac and sea salt and toss until coated. Place in the oven for 10–12 minutes, until they go a beautiful golden brown.

vegetarian hassle free, **gluten free**

Remove from the oven, shake the pan to turn the sprouts over and return to the oven for a further 5 minutes, until the sprouts are cooked through and are lovely and caramelised. You do want that darkened edge as it really adds to the flavour.

While everything's roasting, pick the seeds out of the reserved flesh of the butternut squash. About 10 minutes from the end of cooking, add them to the baking tray and roast with the squash until they are crunchy and delicious.

My Tip
When taking the seeds out use a spoon and then scrape clean with a normal dinner knife to get rid of the tough fibres before cooking.

Finally, make the pea purée. Put the peas into a saucepan and pour boiling water over them. Cook over a high heat for 1–2 minutes, until just defrosted and warm.

Drain the peas and place in a bowl of iced water until cold – this will help them keep their colour. Drain and place in a blender or food processor. Add 3 tablespoons olive oil and blitz until you are happy with the texture, adding more olive oil if necessary. Add a squeeze of lemon juice and a pinch of salt to taste, then set aside until you're ready to serve.

If you want a really fine purée, push through a sieve. However, this should be fine for most needs at home.

To serve, arrange the butternut squash on a large plate and scatter the seeds on top. Serve the roasted garlic to the side for people to squeeze onto the squash if they like, and bring to the table along with the roasties, sprouts and purée.

Vegetarian Hotpot

serves 6–8

Hotpot is a beautiful dish, and this is a vegetarian version that I have served at many corporate functions. It's big, hearty and filling and is great for that Sunday roast dinner.

splash of sunflower oil
1 onion, finely chopped
1 leek, finely chopped
2 carrots, finely chopped
2 celery stalks, finely chopped
2 garlic cloves, finely chopped
½ teaspoon finely chopped rosemary,
  parsley and oregano
350g (approx.) King Edward
  potatoes, finely sliced to the
  thickness of a 10-pence piece
50g unsalted butter, melted, plus
  extra for greasing
○ 100ml vegetable stock
sea salt and black pepper

You will need
1lb loaf tin

Preheat the oven to 180°C/160°C Fan/Gas Mark 4. Grease the inside of the loaf tin liberally and season well.

Heat the oil in a large frying pan over a low heat and slowly sauté the onion, leek, carrots, celery, garlic and herbs together until gently softened, about 5 minutes. The vegetables should be al dente.

Lay two layers of thinly sliced potato in the loaf tin, arranging them up the sides as well. Place one layer of the vegetables over the potatoes, season and repeat. Finish with more potato but tuck in any outside pieces of potato on the top layer. Brush liberally with melted butter, season and pour on the vegetable stock.

Place in the oven and cook for 2 hours until crispy and golden on the top. Leave to cool for a little and turn out. You can slice at the table like a roast and serve with vegetables of your choice.

Puy Lentil Stew with Whole Roasted Celeriac

serves 4–6

This is a wonderful stew, and I love it served with this roasted celeriac, but it's also great on its own or served with the Whole Roast Romanesco Cauliflower with Rich Onion Sauce (page 60). It's very easy and I have deliberately left it soupy so that you have lots of lovely gravy with it.

Celeriac is probably the most ugly of vegetables, so much so that if you serve it at Halloween and call it something suitably horrible like Frankenstein's Brains the kids will eat it just because it's fun. I really enjoy it when roasted whole, as you can either slice it on into 'steaks' or serve it in its whole gnarly state. It has a wonderful woody earthy flavour that is perfect for those autumn and winter evenings.

1 celeriac, 800g-1kg in weight, scrubbed clean
olive oil
10g tarragon, chopped plus extra to serve
4 cloves garlic, crushed
75g butter
sea salt and black pepper

For the puy lentil stew
splash of sunflower oil
50g unsalted butter
1 onion, chopped
2–3 carrots, chopped
1 medium leek, chopped
2 sticks celery, chopped
3 garlic cloves, finely chopped
2 bay leaves
3–4 fresh sage leaves, finely chopped
250g puy lentils
○ *750ml vegetable stock*

You will need
lidded casserole pot or two layers of lightly oiled tin foil

Preheat oven to 180°C/160°C Fan/Gas Mark 4.

Rub the celeriac all over with a little olive oil, sea salt and black pepper and place the celeriac into your casserole pot, rootside up. If using tin foil you need to make a parcel to wrap the celeriac in. Scatter over the herbs and garlic and place the butter on the top then put the lid on, or wrap tightly in tin foil and place on a baking tray.

Cook for about 1 hour 45 minutes-2 hours, until the celeriac is tender all the way through when pierced with a skewer or sharp knife. Cooking times will vary slightly depending on size of your celeriac.

Meanwhile, make the stew. Place all of the ingredients except the lentils, vegetable stock and salt and pepper in a large saucepan and cover with a lid. Cook over a medium heat for about 20 minutes, stirring once or twice but replacing the lid each time. We want to gently cook the vegetables but not brown them and to keep all the lovely juices in the pan.

After 20 minutes add the puy lentils and stir to coat. Add the vegetable stock, stir again and replace the lid. Cook for about 20 minutes, until the lentils are cooked through but still have a little bite. Season as necessary.

To serve, thickly slice the celeriac and place on top of the stew, or serve whole to be carved at the table, scattered with the extra tarragon.

My Tip
Try to chop the vegetables to roughly the same size to ensure even cooking.

Smoked Paprika Bean Stew with Cheesy Thyme Cornbread Topping

serves 4– 6

This is not an authentic cornbread, so to any Americans I apologise, but it works with this smoky bean stew, making a warming one-pot dish. I love using store-cupboard ingredients as we don't always have the time to rush to the shops, and canned beans are particularly useful for both gluten-free and vegetarian dishes. Kidney beans in chilli sauce are widely available and one of my favourite 'cheat ingredients' as they are so versatile and add a really good flavour to dishes.

I use a casserole dish that can go both onto the stove top and in the oven, to keep all the flavours in one pot and save on washing up.

For the smoked paprika bean stew

1 large red onion, chopped
splash of sunflower oil
4 garlic cloves, minced
1 teaspoon smoked paprika
2 x 400g cans kidney beans
   in chilli sauce
1 x 400g can chopped tomatoes
3–4 roasted red peppers from a jar,
   roughly chopped, or 1 whole red
   pepper, chopped
1 x 195g can sweetcorn (160g drained
   weight); or use fresh or frozen
   sweetcorn if you prefer
1–2 teaspoons white wine vinegar,
   to taste
3–4 sprigs of fresh thyme, or
   1 teaspoon dried
10g chopped coriander,
   stalks included
pinch of sea salt (if needed)

For the cheesy thyme cornbread

250g fine cornmeal
75g polenta
2 teaspoons **gluten-free** baking
   powder
½ teaspoon xanthan gum

Preheat the oven to 200°C/180°C Fan/Gas Mark 6.

Gently fry the onion for a couple of minutes in the oil, then add in the minced garlic and smoked paprika. Cook for a further 3–4 minutes, stirring occasionally, until the onion is softened and cooked through.

Remove from the heat and add all the other ingredients. Taste to see if you need any salt, then leave to cool while you make the cornbread.

My Tip
I rarely add salt when using canned ingredients, be very careful as it's often already been added. I taste then add the smallest pinch to balance the flavour at the end of the cooking time. It's better to add a little at the end than add too much.

In a large bowl, combine the cornmeal, polenta, baking powder and xanthan gum.

In a separate bowl combine the thyme, cheese, milk, egg, butter and salt, then pour into the dry ingredients. Mix well but don't overwork; you should have a soft, slightly crumbly dough.

Don't roll out the dough, just gently place it over the stew. It might look a little crumbly in places but don't worry. Place in the oven for around 25– 30 minutes, until the top is golden brown and a skewer inserted into the centre comes away dry.

Serve warm on its own or with a big salad.

3–4 sprigs of fresh thyme,
  leaves picked
50g vegetarian Italian hard cheese,
  grated
100ml milk
1 large egg
50g unsalted butter, melted
pinch of sea salt

Cauliflower Cheese

serves 4

This is one of my lovely mother-in-law Barbara's favourite dishes; it's just a family staple, comforting and warming, especially on those colder winter evenings. You can put in all sorts of flavourings, including curry spices and chilli, and mix in different vegetables – I usually add broccoli and cauliflower, but it's also fab with some leeks or onions. Try to make sure all the vegetables are cut up to the same size so they cook through evenly, and have fun experimenting.

1 medium cauliflower, cut into large florets

For the cheese sauce
4½ tablespoons cornflour
500ml milk, plus 4 tablespoons to make a paste
½ teaspoon sea salt
good grind of black pepper
150g strong Cheddar cheese, grated, plus extra for sprinkling
50g vegetarian Italian hard cheese, grated
50g mozzarella cheese, grated

Preheat the oven to 200°C/180°C/Gas Mark 6.

Cook the cauliflower in boiling water until tender but not cooked through, about 8 minutes (depending on the size of the florets); it's going to cook more in the oven so you don't want it to go to mush. Test with a knife: the stalk should pierce but still show quite a lot of resistance.

Drain and put the cauliflower in a baking dish. I try to use a dish that the cauliflower fits into quite tightly.

While the cauliflower is cooking, make the cheese sauce. Mix the cornflour with the 4 tablespoons of milk until it forms a lump-free paste.

Put the 500ml milk into a saucepan with the salt and black pepper and bring slowly to the boil, stirring so the milk does not scald. As soon as the milk is boiling, add in the cornflour paste and stir quickly until the mixture thickens. Cook through for a further minute and remove from the heat. Immediately add the cheeses and mix in quickly. If they do not all melt, don't worry; they will do so in the oven.

Pour the sauce over the cauliflower, sprinkle with a little extra grated Cheddar and place in the oven for 25–30 minutes, until the top is golden and bubbling. Remove from the oven and leave to sit for about 10 minutes before eating.

My Tips
This can be assembled the day before and left in the fridge overnight for cooking the next day.

Use the cheap grated mozzarella. You can add in different types of cheese to replace the Cheddar; such as blue cheese or a garlic and herb cheese.

Cheat's Vegetarian Chilli

I call this a cheat's chilli because I use the cans of beans in chilli sauce. I love them – it makes this dish so easy to prepare and I can have it on the table within 30 minutes of getting in the door. Ben loves it on jacket potatoes, but it works equally well with rice or loaded onto nachos. I like to keep the vegetables chunky in this dish for texture and I use different-coloured peppers for colour and interest. It makes no difference to the taste unless you add a green pepper which is not as sweet.

2 onions, chopped
2 bird's eye chillies (or whatever chilli you like for heat), finely chopped
splash of sunflower oil
250g flat mushrooms, chopped
3 garlic cloves, finely chopped
○ 1 x 400g can red kidney beans in chilli sauce
○ 2 x 400g cans mixed chilli beans in chilli sauce
1 x 400g can of chopped tomatoes
2 tablespoons tomato paste
1 red pepper, chopped
1 yellow pepper, chopped
1 orange pepper, chopped
150g frozen sweetcorn
squeeze of lemon or lime
sea salt, to taste

In a large saucepan, gently fry the onions and chillies in the oil for about 3–5 minutes, until cooked through but not brown. Mix in the chopped mushrooms and garlic and cook down for a further 3 minutes.

Add in the cans of beans and chopped tomatoes and the tomato paste and continue to simmer for about 5 minutes, stirring to prevent the mixture from sticking.

Mix in the peppers and sweetcorn and cook until these are just tender, about 5 minutes (I do like them to retain some texture). Taste and add salt and a squeeze of lemon or lime. I do this at the end as the cans of beans have salt in them and I don't want to overpower the dish.

You can serve immediately or leave in the fridge to eat the next day. This chilli freezes well too.

My Tip
When chopping really hot chillies, use scissors. That way you don't get chilli on your hands – somehow it always ends up in my eye!

Butterbean and Broccoli Italian-style Bake

serves 6

Dishes we can throw in the oven and prep in less than 10 minutes are my idea of heaven mid-week. This bake relies on ingredients I always have in the house or can very easily source from my local mini supermarket. It's super tasty and can be on the table in a little over 30 minutes.

1 onion, chopped
2 tablespoons olive oil
1 broccoli head, stems included, cut into bite-sized pieces (approx. 250g)
2–3 garlic cloves, minced
15g basil, chopped, leaves and stalks kept separate
50g chopped black olives from jar
50ml brine from olive jar
1 x 400g can chopped tomatoes
150g tomato passata
1 large jar of 700g large butterbeans or cans to make up about 500g drained weight, drained and rinsed
100g mature Cheddar cheese, grated
150g mozzarella cheese, grated
sea salt and black pepper, to taste (be careful: both olives and cheese are salty)

You will need
21cm square baking dish

Preheat the oven to 180°C/160°C Fan/Gas Mark 4. Gently fry the onions in the olive oil until softened but not browned, about 3–5 minutes. Add the chopped broccoli, garlic and basil stalks, stir gently and fry off for another 3–4 minutes.

Add the chopped olives, olive brine, chopped tomatoes, tomato passata and drained butterbeans and stir to combine. Add the chopped basil leaves and season with lots of pepper and a pinch of salt.

Put the mixture into the baking dish, sprinkle evenly with the cheeses and place in the oven for 20–25 minutes, until the cheese is a lovely golden brown and the dish is bubbling.

Remove from the oven and leave for 10–15 minutes to cool a little before serving.

This is lovely served on its own, but with a big salad and The Best Extra Cheesy Extra Garlicky Bread (page 48) it makes a wonderful special meal.

My Tip
This dish is delicious with chopped chilli or chilli flakes added to spice it up.

Crispy Fried Tofu with **Vegetable** Stir Fry

serves 2–4

For years tofu was something that I ate in restaurants but really never cooked. However, I have started to experiment more and more with it, and if treated properly it's a real revelation. I press and freeze it to gain extra texture (see the tip, below).

1½ tablespoons sunflower oil
2–3 cloves garlic, finely sliced
  (or chopped)
1 red chilli, finely sliced (or chopped)
5g minced ginger
5 spring onions, finely sliced (white
  and green pieces kept separate)
1 carrot, finely sliced
75g sugar snap peas, sliced in
  diagonal 0.5cm pieces
125g button mushrooms,
  cut into quarters
2 tablespoons **gluten-free** soy sauce
2 tablespoons **gluten-free** teriyaki
  sauce
2 tablespoons sake
100g beansprouts

For the crispy tofu
1 block of firm plain tofu
3 tablespoons cornflour
½ teaspoon garlic salt
sunflower oil, for frying

Before you start press your tofu. If I'm in a rush, I do this between sheets of kitchen towel and use my pizza stone weighted with a saucepan or plate to press the liquid out. Leave for about 10 minutes.

Cut your tofu into bite-sized squares and toss with the cornflour and garlic salt until well coated. You can deep fry the tofu but I put a little oil into a frying pan and fry off until crispy and golden. Place on kitchen towel and reserve.

Place the 1½ tablespoons sunflower oil in a large seasoned wok or deep non-stick frying pan and heat over a high heat. Add the garlic, chilli, ginger and white part of the spring onions to the hot oil. Stir for 2 minutes, until everything is softened and cooked through but not brown.

Add the carrot and sliced sugar snap peas and continue to stir for about another 2 minutes (depending on how thickly you have cut your vegetables), until the carrot starts to soften.

Add the mushrooms, soy sauce, teriyaki sauce and sake and stir in. Let the mixture bubble for another 2 minutes, until the sauce has reduced a little and the mushrooms are all coated in sauce.

Add in the tofu and keep tossing in the pan until warmed and cooked through. Turn off the heat and mix in the beansprouts. Sprinkle over some of the green parts of the spring onion and serve immediately with plain or egg fried rice.

My Tip
You can use extra firm tofu straight from the packet, but I have found if you press and freeze it first it soaks up the sauce much more effectively and gives you a firmer texture. I wrap my tofu in a clean flannel and weigh it down with a heavy saucepan with a bag of flour in. Leave for an hour or two then slice into 1–1.5cm slabs. Place in a single layer on a baking sheet and freeze overnight. These can be bagged or wrapped the next day and kept frozen for up to a month. When you wish to use, defrost and gently press to expel any remaining water before cooking.

Healthy Spicy Peanut Sauce with **Tofu**

serves 4–6

I first read about using cottage cheese as a sauce base a long time ago but had never tried to do it myself until I was putting this book together. I am now such a fan of this sauce in particular. It's very healthy and easy and really packs a punch for flavour.

For the spicy sauce paste
1 x 5g (0.5cm) chunk of fresh ginger
1 red chilli
10g fresh turmeric (optional)
1 shallot
splash of sunflower oil

For the sauce
1 block of plain tofu
spray of sunflower oil
300g cottage cheese
○ *100g peanut butter (a natural one, the darker brown variety)*
○ *750ml–1 litre vegetable stock*
1 small aubergine, cut into thin halves then into moon shapes
1 small courgette, cut into thin halves then into moon shapes

To garnish (optional)
1 red chilli, finely chopped
5g fresh basil, chopped
unsalted peanuts, chopped

Before you start you need to press your tofu. I do this between sheets of kitchen towel and use my pizza stone weighted with a saucepan or plate to press the liquid out. Leave to drain for about 10 minutes (you can start to prepare your other ingredients in the meantime).

Once the tofu has drained, chop it into bite-sized pieces. Spray a non-stick pan lightly with oil and gently fry off the tofu until golden on all sides. Reserve for use later.

To make the spicy sauce paste, blend the ginger, chilli, turmeric and shallot together to form a paste, using a pestle and mortar. Place in a non-stick frying pan and gently fry off in the splash of oil for about 5 minutes to cook out the raw spices; they will go darker and lose the pungent smell. Be careful not to take a big sniff at the beginning – the chilli will hit you.

In a separate bowl blend (whisk) the cottage cheese until smooth and creamy. Add in the peanut butter and blend until fully incorporated.

Add the cottage cheese and peanut butter mixture to the frying pan with three-quarters of the vegetable stock and stir until combined. Keep bubbling on a gentle simmer and add the aubergine and courgette. Leave to cook for 5 minutes, then add the tofu; you may need to add extra vegetable stock to keep the sauce a nice consistency.

Once the vegetables are cooked, serve immediately with plain boiled rice. I like to decorate with some finely chopped chilli, fresh basil and unsalted peanuts.

My Tip
You can add whatever vegetables you like to this dish, but I would suggest pre-blanching things like cauliflower or using quick-cook vegetables as the sauce does not like to be cooked for too long.

Mexican Night In

serves 5

During the finals for *MasterChef* we got to go to Mexico City. One of our best challenges was cooking in the market and seeing the vast variety of tortillas on offer. I have carried on cooking them at home and we love tortillas and tacos. No matter how you want to serve them, I have listed all the recipes that we, as a family, love best – even if they're not strictly traditional. You can serve some or all components; just pick and choose for a great feast. This is a lovely supper to prepare with your children as it really gets them involved; we have always loved this interactive way of eating. It can get a little messy but it's great fun.

In addition, I really think you should serve some grated cheese like a mild Cheddar or mozzarella and some finely shredded lettuce.

For the stewed black beans
splash of sunflower oil
1 red onion
1 chilli, finely chopped
2 x 380g cans of black beans
* (low salt) in water*
175ml red wine
○ *250ml vegetable stock*
¼ teaspoon ground cumin
¼ teaspoon ground coriander
¼ teaspoon ground cinnamon
1 tablespoon dried mixed herbs
10g coriander, finely chopped,
* plus extra to serve*

Heat the oil and gently sauté the onion and chilli for 3–5 minutes, until the onion is softened.

Drain and rinse the beans from one of the cans and reserve. Put the beans and water from the other can into a food processor with the red wine and stock and blend until smooth. Alternatively, use a stick blender.

Put the black bean smoothie into a saucepan with remaining ingredients, and add the softened onion and chilli. Bring to the boil, then simmer for 10 minutes.

Add in the drained black beans and continue to cook down for 10–15 minutes, until the sauce has nearly all evaporated. You want to be able to spoon the mixture into a taco shell or tortilla. If you are making ahead of time to reheat later, leave a little extra sauce so that the mixture is not too thick. To serve, reheat if necessary (you can do this in a microwave) and sprinkle with a little chopped coriander.

My Tip
I have found that some cans of beans can be very salty so I suggest buying the low-salt or no added salt variety and be very careful with the make of stock you are using if it's bought. If you are worried I would suggest using water, and seasoning with salt at the end.

vegetarian hassle free, **gluten free**

For the tortillas/soft tacos (makes 10)

*250g **gluten-free** masa harina flour*
*½ teaspoon **gluten-free** baking powder*
1 teaspoon sea salt
300–350ml warm water

Or

125g fine cornmeal flour
*125g **gluten-free** plain flour*
*½ teaspoon **gluten-free** baking powder*
1 teaspoon sea salt
juice of 1 lime
250ml–300ml warm water

Combine the flour(s), baking powder and sea salt (and lemon juice, if using) and then gradually add the warm water and mix with your fingers until a dough starts to form and easily comes away from the edge of the bowl. The amount of water will depend on your flour so just take it slow until a dough forms; it should not be sticky.

Form the dough into a ball and remove from the bowl. Using the heel of your hand, knead the dough for 5–7 minutes, until smooth, shiny and bouncy. You will feel it change. Alternatively, use a dough hook on an electric mixer.

Once the dough is ready, cut it into ten equal portions, each weighing about 45g, and roll into balls. Lightly coat in a little gluten-free flour and cover with a clean tea towel to stop them drying out.

Place each tortilla between two sheets of greaseproof paper and roll it to approximately 13cm in diameter. Stack between sheets of greaseproof paper and continue rolling until you have used up all the dough. Alternatively, use a tortilla press.

Heat a non-stick frying pan to medium heat. Place a tortilla in the middle and cook for about 2 minutes on each side, until it has little bubbles of golden brown on it and is light and fluffy. These are best eaten straight away, but you can cover them with a slightly damp tea towel and keep in a warm place for up to 30 minutes.

My Tips

The non-masa harina tortillas are stickier so be careful when peeling them off the greaseproof paper. I found it easiest to remove one side of the greaseproof paper, drop the tortilla in the frying pan and then peel off the other side.

You can get the masa harina flour easily online – it's a traditional cornmeal flour mixed with a little lime to give the distinctive flavour of an authentic taco. Of course you can buy ready-made gluten-free tortillas to save time.

You can easily double or triple up this recipe if needed.

Continued on page 86...

For the fresh tomato salsa

3 ripe tomatoes, chopped
1 banana shallot, finely chopped
1 garlic clove, grated or smashed
2 tablespoons olive oil
10g fresh basil
1 red chilli, seeds and pith removed
  and finely chopped (optional)
squeeze of lemon or lime juice
sea salt

Combine the tomatoes, shallot, garlic, olive oil, basil and chilli and season to taste with sea salt and freshly squeezed lemon or lime juice. This is best made an hour in advance and left in the kitchen, covered, to let the flavours develop.

My Tip
Only you know how much chilli you like so please add as much as you like. If you are really unsure, use Chilli Oil (page 212) and adding a little at a time. The flavour will be slightly different but still lovely.

For the guacamole

2 ripe Hass avocados
1 tablespoon mayonnaise
½ chilli, finely sliced
2 tomatoes, finely chopped
5g coriander, chopped
squeeze of lime juice
sea salt

Mash the avocados using a potato masher and add the mayonnaise, chilli, tomatoes and coriander. Stir to combine and add lime juice and sea salt to taste.

My Tip
Add the lime and mayonnaise as soon as you can to stop the avocados from going brown.

For the quick spicy pickled
  red cabbage

250g red cabbage, finely sliced
250ml red wine vinegar
150g caster sugar
1 red chilli, cut in half to the top
  but not sliced through

Place all the ingredients in a saucepan with 500ml water and bring to the boil. Leave to stand for 5 minutes at least, longer if necessary, until you are happy with the taste. Drain and serve.

My Tip
Leaving the chilli whole means that it can easily be removed when you are happy with the spicing.

For the pepper salad

2 peppers (red, yellow or orange
  or a combination but not green),
  cored and sliced into thin strips
2 garlic cloves, crushed
1 tablespoon mixed dried herbs
splash of olive oil
2 teaspoons red wine vinegar

Place the sliced peppers and garlic into a saucepan with the herbs and the oil, and gently cook for 7–8 minutes, until the peppers are softened but still have a bite. Add in the red wine vinegar and reduce, stirring, for another 2 minutes. Turn off and reserve.

Pasta with Butternut Squash, Cavolo Nero and Roast Red Onion

serves 4

Squash is such a versatile vegetable. In this recipe I have used it to make a lovely rich sauce for the pasta. It works wonderfully well with the kale, making a rich pasta with fabulous autumnal flavours.

½ butternut squash, seeds removed and reserved, round end cut into batons about 1.5cm square (about 400g)

2 red onions, cut into 8–10 wedges

2–3 cloves garlic

1 large chilli, chopped (pith and seeds removed if you prefer a milder heat)

½ lemon, chopped into wedges

1 tablespoon dried mixed herbs

2 tablespoons olive oil

75g cavolo nero, thick stems removed

50ml natural yoghurt

400g **gluten-free** penne pasta, or use my lovely fresh recipe for Perfect Gluten-free Pasta (page 199)

freshly grated vegetarian Italian hard cheese, to serve

sea salt and black pepper

Preheat the oven to 220°C/200°C Fan/Gas Mark 7.

Place the squash, onions, garlic, chilli and lemon onto a baking tray and sprinkle over the dried mixed herbs along with a good seasoning of sea salt and black pepper. Toss in the olive oil until all the ingredients are well coated and place in the oven for 35–40 minutes, until the squash is cooked through and golden on the edges, turning the ingredients half-way through.

Pick out the reserved squash seeds from the pulp, season with a little salt and black pepper and place on a baking tray lined with greaseproof paper. Place this in the oven on a separate shelf from the squash and roast for 7–8 minutes, until golden. Remove and leave to cool.

Place the cavolo nero into a pan of boiling water and cook for about 3–5 minutes, until tender. Drain and reserve.

Once the tray of squash is cooked, remove from the oven and discard the lemon rinds. Put half of the roasted squash, onion, roasted garlic and chilli mixture into a liquidiser, blender or bowl. Add in the natural yoghurt and blend or mash together until you have a purée.

Bring a large pan of well-salted water to the boil, add the pasta and cook for 7–8 minutes, until al dente, then drain.

To serve, toss the cooked pasta into the puréed squash so that it's completely coated. Gently break up the remaining roast squash, onion, garlic and chilli mixture into bite-sized pieces and add to the pasta with the cavolo nero. Mix through and sprinkle the roasted squash seeds over the top of the pasta.

I like to serve this with a grating of vegetarian Italian hard cheese and a good twist of black pepper.

Vegetarian Bolognese

serves 8–10

A good Bolognese sauce is something we probably all eat at least once a month whether with spaghetti or lasagne. It's become as much a staple of our diet as a good pie, I think. I don't like to use meat substitutes, so I really wanted to make a vegetable version of this classic dish that had that feel of heartiness that you want from this great pasta dish. I am really pleased with this and in fact, it's so cost effective and goes such a long way that it's become our standard version. I know the ingredient list looks long but we want to build flavour and it's really a very easy recipe once everything is chopped.

25g dried porcini mushrooms
250ml boiling water
splash of sunflower oil
2 sticks celery, chopped
1 leek, chopped
1 onion, chopped
3 carrots, chopped
2 tablespoons mixed dried herbs
2 bay leaves
4 sprigs of fresh thyme, leaves picked
4 garlic cloves, grated or finely
  chopped
125ml red wine
1 400g can chopped tomatoes
1 x 400g carton tomato passata
1 courgette, chopped
250g white mushrooms
1 teaspoon sugar
***gluten-free** pasta, to serve*
sea salt and black pepper, to taste

Put the dried porcini mushrooms in a jar with the boiling water and leave to one side to soak.

Put the oil, celery, leek, onion, carrots, mixed dried herbs, bay leaves and thyme into a large saucepan with a lid. Gently sauté for 10 minutes, then add the garlic, stir and replace the lid. Leave for another 10 minutes, stirring occasionally to make sure it isn't sticking.

Add in the red wine and stir. Cook until the red wine is all evaporated, stirring continuously.

Drain the dried porcini, reserving the mushrooms. Add the liquid to the saucepan along with the chopped tomatoes and passata; stir and put the lid back on. Chop the dried mushrooms and add to the saucepan along with the courgette and white mushrooms. Stir well.

Add the sugar, salt and black pepper and replace the lid. Simmer for about 10 minutes, stirring. If you feel the ragu is too wet, take the lid off and reduce. Taste – once the courgette is tender and the mushrooms are cooked your ragu will be done.

Serve with a good grating of cheese and a big bowl of pasta.

My Tip
This freezes really well so it's a great one to make and then put some in the freezer for use on those nights when you need something quick. It's also great in lasagne.

Vegan Lasagne

serves 6

This lasagne can be made using the gluten-free cheese sauce that I featured in *Hassle Free, Gluten Free* but for a change I thought I would feature a dairy-free alternative in this recipe.

I am surprised by how much my whole family, including my carnivore husband, loves this dish. As with many lasagnes there is a little bit of love and time needed to put the dish together – I make a base sauce which is cooked down then combined with the other ingredients – but I think it's well worth it.

1 x quantity of Vegan Cheese Sauce (page 210)
250g baby spinach
*approx. 8 **gluten-free** lasagne sheets*

For the base sauce
1 aubergine
½ large red onion (use the other half for the filling)
1 courgette
2 carrots
3–4 garlic cloves
3 tablespoons mixed dried herbs
splash of olive oil
750g tomato passata
sea salt and black pepper

For the filling
½ large red onion, chopped into bite-sized pieces
splash of olive oil
500g chestnut or white mushrooms, roughly chopped
2 garlic cloves, grated or finely chopped

Preheat the oven to 180°C/160°C Fan/Gas Mark 4.

First make the base sauce. Using a food processor or hand grater, grate the aubergine, red onion half, courgette, carrots and garlic cloves. Place in a large saucepan along with the mixed dried herbs, olive oil and a good grind of black pepper. Cover and cook over a low heat until the vegetables are really soft and tender but not coloured, about 20–25 minutes; keep the lid on and stir a couple of times during the process.

In the meantime, prepare the filling. In a separate pan cook off the other red onion half in the oil until softened, then add the mushrooms and garlic. Stir and cook for 3–4 minutes, until the mushrooms are firm but slightly cooked and giving off some juices. Add the chopped courgettes and stir. Leave to cook for another 2–3 minutes, then add the chopped peppers and turn off the heat.

Make your vegan cheese sauce using the recipe on page 210. Then add the spinach to your food processor (you may need to do this in batches) and blend until the spinach is combined into the sauce, which should become a lovely vibrant green. Alternatively, use a stick blender.

Once the base mixture is cooked, add the passata and cook for a further 5 minutes. Add the filling mixture to the base mixture, stir together thoroughly and taste. You may want to add a pinch of salt and some black pepper.

*2 courgettes, chopped into
bite-sized pieces*
*2 red peppers, or a mix of red,
yellow and orange*

You will need
32 x 22cm lasagne dish or similar

Place roughly half of the mixture evenly over the bottom of your lasagne dish, add a layer of gluten-free lasagne sheets and spread evenly with half of the vegan cheese sauce. Repeat the process, finishing with the remaining sauce.

My Tip
Sometimes I have a small bowl of the filling left over when I have compiled my lasagne; it depends on the size of the vegetables you are using. It freezes well or I often use it up with pasta or fish or on a jacket potato.

Place in the oven and cook for 45–50 minutes, until the lasagne sheets are soft and tender when pierced with a sharp knife and the edges are bubbling and brown.

You can serve this lasagne with a big green salad and gluten-free garlic bread. The Best Extra Cheesy Extra Garlicky Bread (page 48) is particularly good.

Pasta with Peas, Broccoli and Pine Nuts

serves 4

This is a great pasta for those healthy days when you are trying to eat green and it's really lovely in the summertime.

250g **gluten-free** *fusilli or similar*
100g broccoli, stalks included, cut into bite-sized pieces
2 tablespoons olive oil
1 garlic clove, minced
½ teaspoon cracked black pepper
160g mangetout, each pod cut into 3 pieces
zest of 1 lemon
75g pine nuts, toasted
1 x quantity of Pea Purée (page 70)
vegetarian Italian hard cheese, grated, to serve
sea salt

Bring a large pan of water to the boil and add the pasta with a good pinch of salt. Cook to the packet instructions.

In a large saucepan fry off the broccoli in the olive oil for 3–4 minutes. Add in the garlic, black pepper and mangetout and stir. Fry for another 2–3 minutes. You don't want to overcook, so leave with some bite.

Add in the lemon zest and turn off the heat.

In a small pan lightly toast the pine nuts. These burn really quickly, so be careful.

Drain the pasta and reserve the cooking liquid. Pour the cooked pasta into the pan with the cooked vegetables, add the pea purée and toss through with half of the toasted pine nuts. If you need extra liquid, add some of the pasta cooking liquid.

Serve sprinkled with the grated cheese and the remaining toasted pine nuts.

My Tip
If you don't have some of the pea purée simply cook some peas and mash or blend. It won't be as fine but it will work.

Sweetcorn and Chilli Risotto

serves 4

Risotto is a lovely meal and wonderful when you have the time to just stand and stir a pot. Sometimes that's perfect but often we need things that aren't quite so time consuming. This version is a lot quicker. You can just leave it to bubble in between adding ingredients, which makes it perfect for me when I am trying to do many things at once.

3 tablespoons vegetable oil
1 large red onion, finely chopped
1 large red chilli, finely chopped
(I use a hot one but that's up to
you; discard the seeds if you don't
like your food too spicy)
3 garlic cloves, minced
250g arborio rice
100ml dry white wine (I use
a Sauvignon Blanc)
○ 1 litre vegetable stock
300g frozen sweetcorn
50g ricotta
50g feta cheese
40g unsalted butter
10g chopped flat-leaf parsley

Heat the oil in a heavy-based saucepan, then fry off the onion and chilli for 2–3 minutes, until the onion just starts to colour.

Add in the minced garlic and cook for another minute, being careful not to burn it.

Put the rice into the saucepan and stir to coat well with the oil, making sure all the grains are coated.

Add 50ml of the wine and all the vegetable stock to the saucepan, stir well and bring to the boil. Reduce the heat to a simmer and cook for 10–12 minutes, until the mixture is creamy and the rice is nearly cooked through. It will look like a thick soup with just a little stock at the top.

Add in the sweetcorn and the rest of the wine and stir until the sweetcorn is cooked and the risotto is thickened, about 1–2 minutes.

Add in the ricotta, feta and butter and stir through. Check the rice. It should have a little bite but be cooked through. Add in the chopped parsley, saving a little for sprinkling on the top if you like, and serve.

My Tip
I use this same technique to make a simple vegetable risotto with peas and asparagus, which works brilliantly too.

vegetarian hassle free, **gluten free**

BBQ Tempeh Bites

serves 2–3

I like the texture of tempeh. This recipe would work really well with tofu, but tempeh is much easier than pressing tofu, so for quick cooking I tend to use it more. You can now buy it in blocks like tofu but I originally bought a number of jars online, which I drain very well before use.

1 jar of tempeh, drained (175g drained weight)
25g cornflour
sunflower oil, for frying
1 x quantity of Spicy BBQ Sauce (page 204)

Cut the tempeh into bite-sized pieces and toss in the cornflour until well covered.

Put enough oil into a large non-stick frying pan to come halfway up the tempeh pieces.

Heat the oil, then gently put the floured tempeh into the frying pan. Fry for about 3 minutes on one side until crispy and golden, then turn over and repeat the process, frying off on the other side for about 2 minutes.

Remove from the pan and place on kitchen towel to drain.

Place in a bowl, cover in BBQ sauce and serve immediately.

My Tip
This technique can be used with any sauce. We like to serve the tempeh with the Asian-style Slaw (page 140) and chips but it's also lovely with a sweet jacket potato and salad.

Crispy Asian-style Pancakes, Peppered Tofu and Stir-Fried Vegetables

makes 3–4
pancakes

We love these crispy-style pancakes. They are just a little different and perfect paired with peppered tofu and stir-fried veg. I also love to serve them with the Asian-style Slaw (page 140), with crispy tofu or with tempeh. These are large pancakes that you fold like a tortilla and fill, so they make a lovely alternative to tortillas and are egg free.

For the pancake batter
225g **gluten-free** white rice flour
30g cornflour
1 teaspoon sugar
1 teaspoon turmeric powder
250ml full-fat coconut milk
1 tablespoon **gluten-free** soy sauce
splash of sunflower oil

For the peppered fried tofu
1 x 280g pack of extra-firm tofu
½ teaspoon black pepper
1½ teaspoons cornflour
2 tablespoons sunflower oil

For the vegetable stir fry
splash of sunflower oil
1 onion, finely chopped
2–3 garlic cloves, grated
1 tablespoon grated ginger
1 carrot, finely sliced
50g white mushrooms, roughly
  chopped (or quartered if small)
4 tablespoons **gluten-free** soy sauce
2 tablespoons rice wine vinegar
1 tablespoon **gluten-free** teriyaki
  sauce
○ 100–200ml vegetable stock
150g beansprouts
1 red pepper, finely sliced
1 chilli, finely sliced (optional)
2 choi sum or Asian-style cabbage

Drain the tofu and chop it into 1cm-square pieces and place on kitchen towel. Cover with more kitchen towel and put a weighted saucepan on top. Leave to stand for at least 30 minutes, pressing down occasionally.

Place all the pancake ingredients (except the oil) in a bowl with about 200ml cold water and whisk together to make a smooth batter. Heat the oil in a non-stick frying pan, then, using a ladle, drop in enough batter to swirl around to the edges of the pan. Cook for about 2 minutes, until golden on one side, flip over and cook until the second side is golden, about 1 minute. Place on a plate and repeat until you have cooked all your pancakes. Cover with a tea towel for up to 1 hour until you are ready to serve.

Combine the tofu with the black pepper and cornflour and toss well to coat. Heat the oil in a large frying pan or wok and fry off for about 5–8 minutes, until the tofu is crispy and golden on all sides. Remove from the pan and place to one side.

Using the same pan, add a splash of oil and fry off the onion for about 2 minutes. Add in the garlic and ginger, fry for 1 minute and then add the carrot, mushrooms, soy sauce, rice wine vinegar, teriyaki sauce and 100ml of the vegetable stock. Cook for another 2 minutes and add in all the rest of the vegetables and more stock if needed. Cook for another 3–5 minutes, until the cabbage is wilted and the vegetables are al dente. Add in the tofu and toss through. Remove from the heat.

To serve, put a large portion of the vegetable and tofu stir-fry onto one half of a pancake and fold the other side over to enclose. Repeat for the remaining pancakes and serve.

My Tip
Use whatever vegetables you like for this, using up whatever you have to hand.

Black Bean Burgers

serves 4

Once Rebecca turned vegetarian it was a real impetus to me to try out new things and get out of a rut with only featuring meat or fish as the main event of any meal. However, I still continued to make burgers, while she would buy a lovely vegetarian patty. I finally realised that I should look into making my own vegetarian version, the way I do with everything else, and these fantastic black bean burgers are the result. I've paired them here with classic Mexican sides, but they're also delicious with any of the sides from the Mexican Night In (page 84) or the Sriracha Mayo Corn Salsa (page 207).

2 x 400g cans of black beans,
drained and rinsed
splash of sunflower oil, plus extra
for frying
1 onion, finely chopped
1 red chilli, finely chopped
(I use hot red)
3 garlic cloves, minced
15g coriander, finely chopped,
stalks included
1 large egg
zest and juice of 1 lime
½ teaspoon salt
4 gluten-free *burger buns, to serve*

For the guacamole mayonnaise
1 small ripe Hass avocado
(320–350g)
½ red chilli, deseeded and
finely chopped
splash of sunflower oil
10g coriander, finely chopped
15g (2–3) spring onions, chopped,
green parts included

Preheat the oven to 180°C/160°C Fan/Gas Mark 4.

Put the black beans onto a baking tray lined with greaseproof paper. Bake in the oven for 10 minutes and then shake them about to turn them over. Bake for another 8–10 minutes; they should still be soft but when pressed have a slightly chalky texture. Leave to cool.

My Tip
When I first made these burgers we loved the flavour but the texture was so mushy that actually it was a bit unpleasant. That's why it's important to take the time to bake the beans and mash with a potato masher rather than use a blender.

Heat the oil in a non-stick frying pan and sauté the onion and chilli over a low–medium heat for about 3 minutes, until clear and cooked through (but try not to brown the onion). Put the minced garlic into the pan and cook for 1 minute more. Remove from the heat and leave to cool a little.

Place the cooled beans into a large bowl and, using a potato masher, mash until they have a coarse texture. Add in the onion mixture, chopped coriander, egg, lime zest and juice and salt and combine well.

Divide into four equal-sized burger patties (about 110g each) and place onto a cling film-lined plate. Chill well for at least an hour.

○ *3 tablespoons mayonnaise*
  splash of smoked chipotle oil
  (optional)
  squeeze of lemon or lime juice

For the elotes-style corn
4 fresh sweetcorn, corn husks
  removed
sunflower oil, for brushing
○ *4 tablespoons mayonnaise*
  200g mozzarella cheese, shredded
  squeeze of lime juice
  pinch of sea salt
○ *sriracha, to taste*

To make the guacamole mayonnaise, roughly chop the avocado flesh and place all the ingredients in a large bowl and combine well.

To make the elotes-style corn, brush the corn lightly with the oil, place on a BBQ and cook until roasted and blackened in places. Alternatively, preheat the oven to 240°C/220°C Fan/Gas Mark 9 and cook the corn for 20–25 minutes, turning to ensure that all sides are cooked.

In a bowl combine the mayonnaise, mozzarella, lime juice and salt and combine. Add sriracha to taste. Once the corn is blackened, remove from the heat and coat thickly in the mayonnaise dressing. Serve immediately.

When you are ready to cook the burgers, put a little oil in a non-stick pan and fry until golden brown, about 3 minutes. Flip and repeat. Remove and serve with whatever sides you prefer.

sides and salads

This book has taught me so much. Traditionally, the centrepiece for any meal I served has always been a big joint of meat or whole fish, with vegetables and salads arranged around to support that centre. However, the recipes in this chapter reflect how my cooking is changing. I now bring a big platter of vegetables to the table as a centrepiece, including roasted squash and vegetables that can be carved at the table in the same way you would a joint of beef. These dishes are perfect to pair with any number of proteins, or as sides to any of the dishes in the previous chapter, or you can mix and match to create a delicious veggie feast.

Clockwise from top left: Pea and Black Garlic Potato Cakes (page 120), Carrot, Cardamom and Orange Purée (page 109), Brussels Sprout Tops with Toasted Almonds, Lemon and Black Pepper (page 135) and Hasselback Carrots with Thyme and Cheese Gratin (page 108)

Hasselback Carrots
with **Thyme** and
Cheese Gratin

serves 6

Every roast dinner has to have carrots, from the tiny new season ones picked from the garden to the bigger winter vegetable. This dish is based on those big carrots, and is a real celebration of this humble vegetable which is one of my very favourites.

6 large carrots
75g unsalted butter
○ *vegetable stock to cover*
  (approx. 300ml)
½ garlic bulb, left intact
10 stalks of fresh thyme
freshly ground black pepper

For the gratin
15g flat-leaf parsley, chopped
  and stalks reserved
15g vegetarian Italian hard cheese
*40g **gluten-free** breadcrumbs*
  (I make my own or use Mrs
  Crimble's)
good grind of black pepper

Preheat the oven to 180°C/160°C Fan/Gas Mark 4.

Peel the carrots and top and tail them. Place a wooden spoon face down on your chopping board, put the carrot next to it and using a sharp knife cut into the carrot until you hit the back of the spoon – this way you should ensure even-depth cuts without cutting all the way through. Make a cut every few millimetres, keeping the cuts as equal as possible until you have cut all down the carrot.

Place the carrots into a roasting tin with the butter and vegetable stock. The stock should reach the top of the carrots, only just covering them; you might need a little more or less depending on the size of your tin.

Add the garlic, thyme, black pepper and the reserved parsley stalks from the gratin ingredients, and place in the oven for 30 minutes.

My Tip
You can prepare the carrots up to this stage the day before you want to serve them, if necessary. On the day just continue as per the below.

Combine all the gratin ingredients well.

Remove the carrots from the oven. Sprinkle with the gratin ingredients and return to cook for a further 10–15 minutes; the carrots should retain their shape but fan out and be golden brown on top.

My Tip
Please be careful with your stock. Stock cubes and ready-made stock can be incredibly salty and when reduced, as in this recipe, result in a horrible finished dish. I would suggest using homemade vegetable stock or any water you have strained from boiling carrots or dark greens for another recipe instead of a stock cube when reducing because of this.

vegetarian hassle free, **gluten free**

Carrot, Cardamom and Orange Purée

serves 4–6

Making a carrot purée is very easy and it really can add something special to your dish. That sweep of beautiful colour and flavour can just lift what you are cooking. This purée of classic flavours works beautifully when served with fish but also as an accompaniment to most vegetable dishes. I serve it topped with the Hasselback Carrots with Thyme and Cheese Gratin (page 108) and drizzled with Carrot-top Pesto (page 110) to make a real centrepiece focused on carrots.

4 large winter carrots, peeled and chopped
4 green cardamom pods, crushed, seeds removed and shells discarded
250ml fresh orange juice
15g chopped flat-leaf parsley
sea salt, to taste

Place all the ingredients except the salt into a saucepan with 250ml water and bring to the boil. Reduce the heat and simmer until the carrots are really soft and tender.

Drain and reserve the liquid. Place the carrots into a blender, or use a stick blender, and blitz until you have a smooth purée, adding a little of the cooking liquid if required.

My Tip
You can push the carrots through a sieve using the back of the spoon if you don't have a blender.

Season with salt to taste. This purée can be made the day ahead and reheated when you need it.

Carrot-top Pesto

makes
150–200ml

If you have the pleasure of growing your own carrots or can buy them with the lovely green tops on, please don't waste them – they are wonderful made into this earthy pesto. You can use this to dress dishes and salads; it's great on new potatoes for a different potato salad. Combine this with the Hasselback Carrots with Thyme and Cheese Gratin (page 108) and the Carrot, Cardamom and Orange Purée (page 109) and you have a wonderful dish that is a real centrepiece on a vegetarian spread.

2 bunches of carrot tops (about 60g), well washed, leaves picked and stalks discarded
20g flat-leaf parsley, leaves picked
1 garlic clove
20g hazelnuts
100–125ml sunflower oil
1–2 tablespoons lemon juice
sea salt, to taste

Prepare a saucepan of boiling water, a bowl of iced water and a sieve or drainer.

Plunge the carrot tops and parsley leaves into the boiling water for a minute. Drain well and plunge immediately into the iced water. This will set the lovely deep green colour. Leave until chilled. Drain well and squeeze to get rid of all the excess water.

Place into a liquidiser with the garlic, hazelnuts, 100ml of the oil and 1 tablespoon of the lemon juice and combine well. Alternatively, use a stick blender. You may need to add a little extra oil to get a good thick pesto sauce.

Taste and add salt and extra lemon juice if required.

vegetarian hassle free, **gluten free**

Swede Fondant

serves 4 (makes
12–16 fondants)

Swede is a wonderful vegetable and I do try to use it
in many different ways. These lovely fondants are the
perfect accompaniment to a veggie feast.

250g (approx.) swede
50g unsalted butter
3–4 sprigs of fresh thyme
grind of cracked black pepper
○ *150ml (approx.) vegetable stock*
sea salt (if the stock is unsalted)

Preheat the oven to 180°C/160°C Fan/Gas Mark 4.

Trim the swede into a rough block and then cut into batons like thick
chips about 6 x 1.5cm deep (note that this is not an exact measurement,
just a rough guide).

Put the swede into a pan with the butter and thyme, and sprinkle over
cracked black pepper and some salt if the stock is unsalted. It makes life
easier if you can have a pan that goes from the stove top to the oven, but
you can transfer from the pan to an ovenproof dish if you need to.

Fry off in the pan on one side until the swede is golden. Do this slowly
(it can take 5 minutes) as the sugars in the swede can burn quickly. Turn
over (if you need to swap pans do it now) then add in the vegetable stock
until it comes to the top of the swede; the amount of stock required will
depend on the size of your pan.

Place in the oven for 25–30 minutes, until soft and tender. If you
are using it next day, leave it in the remaining liquid and refrigerate.

Serve golden-side up. There should be 3–4 fondants per person.

My Tip
These can be made the day before and just put in the oven to reheat on the day.

Swede Casserole with **Maple Syrup** and **Walnuts**

This recipe definitely brings a different aspect to the humble swede and you can cook it the day before and simply reheat it or put it in the microwave if you want. This is a great side dish served with the Vegetarian Hotpot (page 74), and I have paired it with the waffles as a savoury brunch option.

unsalted butter, for greasing
1 medium swede, chopped
2 fresh bay leaves
200ml double cream
200ml milk
1 tablespoon maple syrup
50g chopped walnuts (or pecans
*   if you prefer)*
sea salt and black pepper

You will need
medium baking dish (I use
*   a 25 × 17cm dish)*

Preheat the oven to 180°C/160°C Fan/Gas Mark 4. Grease the dish with butter.

Put the chopped swede into a saucepan with the bay leaves, cream, milk and a pinch of salt and black pepper. Bring to the boil, then reduce the heat and simmer slowly for about 20 minutes, until the swede is soft and tender. Don't be tempted to add more liquid.

Once the swede is soft and tender, take off the heat and remove the bay leaves. Mash the swede in the cream and milk mixture; the swede won't be completely smooth and will keep some texture but get rid of the big lumps if you wish.

Add the maple syrup, season with more salt and black pepper if needed and stir to combine. Put into your baking dish, sprinkle over the chopped walnuts and place in the oven for 20 minutes, until golden. Remove from the oven and serve.

My Tip
I like the addition of maple syrup but be careful not to overdo it as it can quickly turn from a savoury side dish to something that verges on dessert. Having said that, in America they serve pumpkin with marshmallow on top with turkey, so it really is down to personal taste.

Roasted Swede
Boulangères-style

serves 6

I grew up thinking swede was only ever served when it had been boiled and mashed with lots of butter and black pepper, and on special days with carrot too. That is totally delicious and still something I serve with my roast dinners; however, I have been experimenting with this vegetable. I love it, it's versatile and goes with big-flavoured dishes.

1 medium swede, peeled and chopped into thin slices
1 red onion, cut into thin rings
7–8 sprigs of fresh thyme
○ 700ml vegetable stock (to cover)
50g butter
splash of Chilli Oil (page 212; I like to use the smoked hotter version for this)
100g **gluten-free** breadcrumbs
25g vegetarian Italian hard cheese
sea salt

You will need
medium-sized roasting dish (I use a 25 x 17cm dish)

Preheat the oven to 180°C/160°C Fan/Gas Mark 4.

Start by placing a layer of swede, followed by a layer of red onion, into your roasting dish. Strip some thyme leaves over and continue layering until you have used all the vegetables, finishing with a layer of swede.

Strip some more thyme leaves over the top and fill to the top of the vegetables with vegetable stock. Dot with the butter, drizzle over some chilli oil and sprinkle with a little salt.

Combine the breadcrumbs and hard cheese and sprinkle over the top. Place in the oven for about 2 hours; you want the sauce to really thicken and the swede to be wonderfully soft.

Remove from the oven and leave to cool for about 10 minutes. Serve when warm.

My Tip
You can make this a day in advance and put it in the fridge. Just gently reheat the next day for 20 minutes in a low oven; or you can microwave if you are making a roast dinner and oven space is tight.

vegetarian hassle free, **gluten free**

Turnip and Sweet Potato Mash

serves 6

These two vegetables are so different but together they just work. This pairs wonderfully with the Hassleback Carrot with Thyme and Cheese Gratin (page 108).

350g turnip, cut into cubes
350g sweet potato, cut into cubes
2 garlic cloves, chopped
knob of unsalted butter
10g flat-leaf parsley, chopped
sea salt and black pepper

My Tip
Cut the sweet potato a little bigger than the turnip as it tends to cook a little more quickly; it will make a difference to the texture not the taste.

Put the turnip, sweet potato and garlic into a saucepan of water and bring to the boil; turn down the heat and simmer for 6–7 minutes, until tender. Remove from the heat and drain.

Add the butter and mash together. You can leave some lumps in this – it doesn't need to be a purée.

Stir in the chopped parsley and season with salt and pepper.

Roasted Baby Turnips in Balsamic Vinegar

serves 6

Here's something a little different – turnips are so often the forgotten vegetable, I think, but their peppery crisp flavour is wonderful and really brings something special to the plate. These are very easy – you can roast them the day before and just reheat them if you need to. The whole vegetable looks so pretty glazed on the plate.

6 baby turnips, peeled, roots
    removed and cut straight so
    they stand up
2 tablespoons olive oil
5g fresh thyme, leaves picked
3 tablespoons good balsamic vinegar
25g unsalted butter
sprinkle of sea salt

Preheat the oven to 200°C/180° Fan/Gas Mark 6. Lay out two sheets of tin foil in a cross shape, making sure you have enough tin foil to wrap the turnips up.

Place the turnips root-side down on the tin foil and put the olive oil and thyme around. Drizzle over the balsamic vinegar and put a knob of butter on top of each turnip. Sprinkle with salt and place in the oven for 2 hours until soft and tender.

Remove from the oven, drizzle with the lovely sticky glaze and serve.

My Tip
If you can't get baby turnips you can buy larger ones and cut them into equal-sized segments.

vegetarian hassle free, **gluten free**

Sautéed Turnip Tops with Leeks and Cheese

serves 2

Turnip tops are another vegetable that we ate when I was younger which have come back into shops recently. They have a really distinctive mustard flavour. You can gently blanch the leaves like spinach, and they are wonderful but this is something a little different; it's richer, and uses all the tops, which is great as I hate waste. It also takes less than 15 minutes to cook, which is an added bonus.

350g turnip tops
1 large leek, trimmed and washed (approx. 175g)
25g unsalted butter
5–6 sprigs of fresh thyme, leaves picked
1 tablespoon mascarpone cheese
2 tablespoons vegetarian Italian hard cheese
sea salt and black pepper, to taste

Wash the turnip tops well and strip the leaves from the stalks. Reserve the tender thinner stalks and discard the woody centre stalk. Chop the thin stalks finely. Reserve the leaves.

Cut the leek in half and slice into thin half-moons. Place in a saucepan with the chopped stalks, butter and thyme and gently stir for about 3–5 minutes, until the leeks, stalks and thyme are wilted and the stalks are cooked but still firm.

Add in the leaves and stir to wilt for about 1 minute.

Remove from the heat and stir in the cheeses. Taste and season with salt and black pepper. Serve immediately while hot.

My Favourite Minted Peas

serves 6

Fresh or frozen, I think this is one of my favourite recipes for this humble vegetable. It really adds a little extra, for very little effort.

1 shallot, finely chopped
25g unsalted butter
10g mint leaves, picked and
    finely chopped
○ 1 vegetable stock cube
100ml boiling water
250g fresh or frozen peas

In a frying pan, gently fry off the shallot in the butter for 2–3 minutes, until softened and cooked. Add in half the chopped mint and gently cook for another minute.

Dissolve the vegetable stock cube in the boiling water and add to the pan with the onion and butter.

Put in the peas and bring to the boil for about 2 minutes, until the peas are just cooked and still fresh, bright green and tender.

Remove from the heat and add in the rest of the fresh mint. Reserve a little if you want for garnish.

Serve immediately. You can season with pepper if you like.

My Tip
These work well when served with a little stock or gravy, which makes a really lovely side with most of the vegetarian mains in this book.

Top to bottom: · · · · ·
Broccoli with Smoked Chipotle Oil and Toasted Almonds (page 122), My Favourite Minted Peas (page 118) and Turnip and Sweet Potato Mash (page 115)

vegetarian hassle free, **gluten free**

Pea and Black Garlic Potato Cakes

makes 6–8

These little potato cakes are meltingly soft and delicious but packed full of flavour. They make a great supper or brunch dish with a crispy fried egg.

300g cold mashed potato
5–6 black garlic cloves, mashed into a purée (you can use a knife)
○ 40g mayonnaise (or vegan mayonnaise)
200g peas, cooked and cooled
10g basil
squeeze of lemon juice
sunflower oil, for frying
sea salt, to taste

Place all the ingredients except the oil in a large bowl and use a potato masher to combine them well. Some peas will get smashed – that's okay. Make sure the black garlic in particular does not clump but is spread throughout the mix.

In the bowl, section out the number of portions you need (I usually make between six and eight).

Heat a little oil in a non-stick frying pan. It's important to not use too much as the potato cakes can soak up oil and split apart. Gently drop a portion of the potato cake into the frying pan, squash into a patty using a fish slice and fry for about 2–3 minutes, until golden brown and crispy. Turn over and repeat.

These are lovely served as a side to a meal but we really like to add a little more oil to the pan after you have cooked all the potato cakes and fry off some eggs to eat with them.

My Tip
A little tub of black garlic is a great thing to keep in the fridge. It keeps for ages and you can use it to add into pastas, or roasted vegetables, to give just that little extra. Or use it as in this dish with a little pea and potato.

vegetarian hassle free, **gluten free**

Sweet Sprouting
Cauliflower Salad

serves 4–6

I know this salad sounds a bit bonkers but it's different and it's great as a light lunch or a side as part of veggie tapas feast or buffet. I am a huge fan of pickling and this is similar to a recipe from my first book, but used in a different way.

175g sweet sprouting cauliflower
125g baby spinach, roughly chopped
1 pack of spring onions, finely sliced
100g baby plum tomatoes, chopped
  into 4
10g flat-leaf parsley, finely chopped
2 tablespoons olive oil
25g pistachios, roughly chopped
sea salt

For the pickle
100g caster or granulated sugar
125ml white wine vinegar

Cut the stalk off the cauliflower and reserve the florets. Chop the stalks into bite-sized pieces and place in a small saucepan with the sugar, white wine vinegar and 250ml water. Bring to the boil and simmer for about 3 minutes. Take the pan off the heat, remove the cauliflower stalk and set aside. (You can leave the cauliflower stalk in the pickle if you would like a stronger flavour; taste after about 5 minutes and remove or leave until you are happy.)

Put the chopped spinach, spring onions, tomatoes, and parsley in a large bowl and add the pickled cauliflower stalks.

Take 125g of the pickling liquor, put it back into the saucepan and bring to the boil. Add the olive oil. Stir to combine and pour over the spinach salad. Toss to combine well and add in the raw cauliflower florets.

Sprinkle over the chopped pistachio nuts, add salt to taste, and serve immediately.

Broccoli with Smoked Chipotle Oil and Toasted Almonds

serves 6

I am very lucky that all of my children have always loved vegetables. I think growing up with a grandad who grew his own and who took the children out to pick and plant things really made them appreciate them and I have always served them with all meals. However, Ben's love of broccoli is sometimes funny and sometimes irritating, in that he eats it by the stalk, raw. Consequently, I often go to the fridge to find it gone and we have none for dinner. This recipe is so simple and combines two of his best-loved things: very spicy food and his favourite vegetable.

40g almond flakes
1 head of broccoli, split into florets
drizzle of smoked Chilli Oil
(page 212)
pinch of sea salt flakes
chopped fresh chilli (optional)

Toast the flaked almonds in a saucepan over a high heat, tossing regularly until they are a lovely golden colour.

Blanch the broccoli and drain. Toss it in the chipotle oil and sprinkle over the lightly toasted almonds, a pinch of sea salt flakes and the finely chopped red fresh chilli, if using.

vegetarian hassle free, **gluten free**

Broccoli Roasted with **Lemon** and **Pine Nuts**

serves 4–6

Broccoli is a vegetable most people eat and it's nice to jazz it up and serve it a little differently occasionally. I love to serve this with the Veggie Sunday Lunch (page 70), but it's also a real favourite with the Warm Harissa-spiced Butternut Squash, Chickpeas and Spinach Salad (page 66).

1 large broccoli head (approx. 400g)
50g pine nuts

For the dressing
3 tablespoons olive oil, plus extra
*   to serve*
zest of 1 lemon
juice of ½ lemon, plus extra to serve
1 teaspoon sea salt
good grind of black pepper

Preheat the oven 180°C/160°C Fan/Gas Mark 4.

Cut the florets off the broccoli, working up the stalk to try to save as much of it as you can. Take off any leaves and reserve. Carefully peel the stalk.

Put the stalk, leaves and florets on a roasting tray and sprinkle over the dressing ingredients. Toss until the broccoli is coated, then place in the oven for 15 minutes.

Remove from the oven, take off the leaves if they are crispy and cooked and add the pine nuts. Toss everything to coat again, turning the broccoli over, then cook for a further 10 minutes, until golden brown and toasty.

Taste and squeeze over a little more lemon juice and olive oil if needed. Dress with the crispy leaves.

You can serve this either warm or cold as part of a buffet.

My Tip
Please don't waste the stalks and leaves of broccoli or cauliflower. They really are delicious and it's great to use the whole vegetable.

BBQ Watermelon with **Roasted Feta** Salad

serves 4–6

A lovely fresh salad that I prepare on my BBQ when watermelons are plentiful. You can also cook the watermelon on a griddle indoors if we have one of our predictable rainy days.

5g basil, chopped, plus extra
  for dressing
1 x 200g block feta cheese
2 tablespoons Chilli Oil (page 212)
1 watermelon (see Tip)

You will need
28 x 18cm roasting dish
griddle pan or bbq

Preheat the oven to 180°C/160°C Fan/Gas Mark 4.

Put the basil and the feta block into a small roasting dish, drizzle over the chilli oil and place in the oven for 20 minutes.

Place the watermelon on a hot griddle pan or BBQ and cook for about 3 minutes, until you have nice black grid marks. Turn and repeat, then place onto a plate to rest while the feta cooks. Reserve any juice that runs from the melon.

Cut each melon piece into quarters.

Once the feta is cooked (it should be melting), stir it into the chilli oil and basil. Combine half of the mixture with any reserved melon juice and place on a plate.

Arrange the melon slices on top and then spoon over the rest of the melted feta. Sprinkle with a little chopped fresh basil and serve.

This can be served warm or cold on the day you made it.

My Tip
I use a small seedless watermelon that I cut into rounds about 1.5cm thick and griddle whole circles. Alternatively, you can use a bigger melon but leave the rind on when cooking.

vegetarian hassle free, **gluten free**

Bombay Potatoes

serves 4–6

Easy to make, with loads of flavour, these are great with a tomato and onion salad for lunch but also as part of a big Indian feast.

750g potatoes, peeled and cut
  into cubes
1 large onion, sliced into half-rounds
50ml sunflower oil
1 red chilli, finely chopped
1 teaspoon black mustard seeds
$\frac{1}{2}$ teaspoon turmeric
$2\frac{1}{2}$ teaspoons garam masala
$\frac{1}{2}$ teaspoon sea salt
4 large tomatoes, finely chopped
2 large garlic cloves, grated
10g coriander, chopped, stalks
  included
squeeze of lemon juice

Parboil the potatoes until just tender and drain well. Leave in the colander to ensure there is no water left on them.

Place the sliced onion into a frying pan with the oil and cook slowly for 6–8 minutes, until soft and tender; it can be a little golden but not burnt.

Add in the finely chopped chilli, black mustard seeds, turmeric, garam masala and salt. Stir well and continue to cook for a couple of minutes.

Combine the chopped tomatoes and garlic and add to the pan. Stir in the potatoes and cook for another 5–6 minutes, until the potatoes are soft and cooked through. Try to keep them whole, but if a few of them start to break up a little it's not a problem.

Add in the chopped coriander, reserving a little for decoration if you like. Add lemon juice to taste and serve.

Cheese and Potato Bake

serves 4

This is a really great dish to serve everyday, but it works beautifully for special occasions too. If you like Dauphinoise you will love this, but it is so much easier than slicing all those potatoes, and it's another dish you can prepare the day before and cook on the day. I love to serve these with the Whole Roast Romanesco Cauliflower with Rich Onion Sauce (page 60).

2 onions, finely sliced
50g unsalted butter, plus extra
  for greasing
2–3 cloves garlic, finely grated
2 tablespoons mixed dried herbs
700g cold mashed potato (with no
  butter or seasoning)
½ teaspoon sea salt
½ teaspoon white pepper
200g strong Cheddar cheese, grated
200g mascarpone cheese

Preheat the oven to 180°C/160°C Fan/Gas Mark 4. Grease a baking dish with butter.

Gently fry off the onions in the butter for about 3 minutes. Add in the garlic and mixed dried herbs and gently fry for another 1–2 minutes, making sure not to burn the garlic and keeping the onions soft but not darkened. Leave to one side to cool slightly.

Put the onion mixture in a bowl with all the remaining ingredients and combine well so that there are no lumps of cheese.

Put the mixture into the baking dish and rough up the top with a fork. Place in the oven for about 45 minutes, until the top is golden brown and crispy.

These work wonderfully well with almost anything, but we especially love them with a roasted centrepiece such as a whole cauliflower.

My Tip
Use a specialist potato for mashing. King Edwards and Russets are my favourites but just search online to see which varieties you can use.

vegetarian hassle free, **gluten free**

Easy Dauphinoise

serves 4

This is a true family favourite, and now I have a food processor and a mandoline I can easily slice potatoes quickly. However, sometimes at home you want a method that involves quick chopping and throwing in, so this is a simplified recipe that I really like. It makes a lovely dish served with a green salad or a wonderful side in a veggie feast.

750g new potatoes, washed but skins left on, cut into quarters or bite-sized pieces
300ml double cream
300ml milk
3–4 garlic cloves garlic, grated
sea salt

Preheat the oven to 180°C/160°C Fan/Gas Mark 4.

Put the potatoes into a saucepan with the cream, milk, garlic and a pinch of salt. If the liquid does not quite cover the potatoes, add a little more milk. Stir and bring to the boil, then simmer for 5–7 minutes, until tender. Be careful – this can catch on the bottom of the saucepan, so it's best to give it a gentle stir while simmering.

Tip carefully into a baking dish and place in the oven for 25–30 minutes, until bubbling and golden on top.

My Tip
This dish is best served warm. I often make these in the morning or the day before and cover with tin foil, then warm through in the oven to serve.

Beetroot Salad with **Horseradish, Orange** and **Walnut**

serves 4–6

I hated beetroot as a child. I remember being offered a beetroot sandwich by my wonderful grandad, white bread stained purple with vinegar from a jar of beetroot. I am sure that anyone else who grew up in the 1970s will remember every salad being overtaken by the stuff, but since *MasterChef* I have had a revelation. Fresh beetroot is wonderful. It's so versatile and the earthy flavours pair so well with lots of beautiful autumnal ingredients.

This quick salad is lovely and uses the leaves of the beetroot, too.

300g fresh beetroot, peeled and cut into equal-sized wedges
splash of olive oil
pinch of sea salt
good grind of black pepper
75g beetroot leaves, chopped
6 orange segments, pith removed
15g chopped walnuts, to garnish

For the dressing
2 tablespoons olive oil
1 tablespoon horseradish sauce
squeeze of lemon juice
pinch of sea salt

Preheat the oven to 180°C/160°C Fan/Gas Mark 4.

Place the beetroot onto a sheet of tin foil big enough to make a parcel for roasting and sprinkle with the oil, salt and pepper. Fold over the tin foil to make a parcel. Place in the oven for 30–40 minutes, until soft and tender. Remove and open the parcel to let the beetroot cool.

Make the dressing by combining the olive oil, horseradish and lemon juice in a bowl. Season with salt to taste.

Place the cooked warm beetroot in a bowl with the beetroot leaves, orange segments and walnuts. Pour on the dressing and toss well to coat thoroughly. Serve immediately.

Sprinkle on the chopped walnuts and serve.

My Tips
I would also recommend using gloves to peel the beetroot (unless it's Halloween) to avoid staining your fingers!

If you don't have beetroot leaves, you can use fresh spinach instead.

Goat's cheese works very well crumbled over this salad.

Beetroot Leaf Crisps

serves 2–4

If you are lucky enough to get access to beetroot with the beautiful leaves fresh, please don't waste them. They make a delicious salad simply dressed with some lemon, olive oil and salt. Or I love to make them into crisps to serve with the Roast Beetroot with Horseradish (page 131) or any dish where you are serving beetroot to add interest to the plate.

sunflower oil, for frying
8–10 large fresh beetroot leaves,
* well washed and dried*
sprinkle of sea salt

Fill a heavy-based saucepan one-third full with oil and heat to a temperature of 180°C. If you don't have a thermometer, simply drop a cube of gluten-free bread into the pan; if it sinks then rises, bubbling gently, your oil is hot enough. Alternatively, use a deep fat fryer.

Please make sure the leaves are 100 per cent dry, otherwise the oil will spit and burn you.

Place a sheet of kitchen towel onto a plate.

Gently drop a leaf into the oil and turn over after 30 seconds. Cook for a further 30 seconds, then remove and place onto the kitchen towel. Repeat the process until all your leaves are crispy and still a lovely dark green and purple colour.

Gently turn the leaves over to drain as much oil off as possible. Sprinkle with a little sea salt and serve.

My Tip
This technique is also wonderful for making kale crisps.

Roast Beetroot with Horseradish

serves 4-6

This recipe with horseradish is a real favourite. Both flavours are strong but I feel they really complement each other.

300g fresh beetroot, peeled and cut into equal-sized wedges
6–8 sprigs of fresh thyme
50g unsalted butter
○ *2 tablespoons horseradish sauce*
drizzle of olive oil
sea salt and black pepper, to taste

Preheat the oven to 200°C/180° C Fan/Gas Mark 6. Place a large sheet of tin foil onto a baking tray, making sure it's big enough to make a sealed envelope for the beetroot.

Place all the ingredients into the tin foil and seal, leaving a pocket of air inside.

Place in the oven and cook for 50–60 minutes, until the beetroot is soft and tender. Remove from the oven, pour all the lovely beetroot infused horseradish and oils from the tin foil over the beetroot, and serve.

My Tip
You can add another spoonful of the horseradish sauce to the hot beetroot to intensify the flavour if you like.

Beetroot and Apple Coleslaw

serves 6–8

Coleslaw is a huge family favourite when it is homemade and this is one of my go-to sides, with the added benefit that it is easily thrown together.

225g fresh raw beetroot, peeled
225g Bramley apples
○ 150g mayonnaise
75g extra-virgin olive oil
squeeze of lemon juice
sea salt and black pepper, to taste

Grate the beetroot, using gloves to avoid staining your hands.

Grate the apples, leaving the skins on, and discard the cores. Working quickly to avoid the apple from browning, combine all the ingredients in a large bowl. Season and serve.

Top to bottom:
Asian-style Slaw (page 140),
Beetroot and Apple Coleslaw
(page 132) and Honey and
Mustard Brussels Sprout
Coleslaw (page 134)

vegetarian hassle free, **gluten free**

Honey and Mustard Brussels Sprout Coleslaw

serves 6–8

We love this version of a traditional coleslaw. It uses lovely raw sprouts and is not heavy with mayonnaise if you are looking for something a little lighter. This slaw works wonderfully with any buffet-style dinner or roasted veggie platter over the autumn/winter season.

350g raw sprouts, trimmed
200g carrot, grated
1 onion, finely sliced

For the dressing
175ml rapeseed oil or olive oil
75ml white wine vinegar
○ 2 tablespoons wholegrain mustard
pinch of sea salt
2–3 tablespoons runny honey

Finely slice the sprouts. This is most easily done using a food processor on the thin slicing disc, which will take seconds, but you can do it on the slicing bit of a stand-up grater or by hand.

Add the sprouts to a large bowl, with the grated carrot and onion.

Mix the dressing ingredients together, adding the honey last and tasting as you do so. Different vinegar brands will have different acidity levels so just taste as you add the honey until you are happy.

My Tip
You can use golden syrup if you don't like the very distinctive flavour of honey but want the sweetness it brings to the coleslaw.

Combine the dressing with the vegetables and leave for an hour before serving to absorb the flavours.

This salad should be eaten on the day it's made.

Brussels Sprout Tops with Toasted Almonds, Lemon and Black Pepper

serves 4

I think that, because my dad has always grown fabulous vegetables I have grown up eating Brussels tops, but only recently have I seen them for sale in the shops, either as a separate vegetable or as part of the sprouts on stalks that are now sold in most places. Mum always cooked them like any other cabbage, and they are delicious just blanched and served covered with gravy next to your favourite roast, but this recipe is something I cook at home. It can be served warm or cold, making it one of those wonderfully versatile dishes we all need especially at Christmas.

400g Brussels sprout tops
75g flaked almonds

For the dressing
3 tablespoons olive oil
2–3 tablespoons lemon juice
½ teaspoon freshly cracked
  black pepper
sea salt, to taste

Strip the green leaves from any of the tougher stalks of the sprouts; you may need to discard some of the tough outer leaves. If you have a large sprout in the middle, cut it into half so it cooks evenly.

Place in a large pan and cover with water, season well with salt, and bring to the boil. Simmer for 3–5 minutes until tender, then drain.

Meanwhile, place the flaked almonds in a small pan and gently toast them until golden; be careful they do burn easily.

Place the sprouts in a large bowl with the toasted almonds, cover with the dressing ingredients and toss together well. Adjust the salt and pepper if you need to, and serve.

My Tip
If you buy the stalk of Brussels sprouts with the cabbage tops on, take the tiny little Brussels off the top and mix them into this dish. They are so sweet and delicious – please don't waste them.

Courgette Ribbon Salad with Pesto and Tomatoes

serves 4–6

You know those wonderful summer days when you have a glut of warm tomatoes from the garden and so many courgettes? For these, this is the perfect salad – so easy to prepare, with vibrant colours and lovely and fresh.

2 medium courgettes, cut into
  ribbons using a vegetable peeler
100g cherry or plum tomatoes,
  cut into quarters

For the pesto
40g fresh basil
125g vegetarian Italian hard cheese,
  freshly grated
125ml extra-virgin olive oil
75g toasted pine nuts
3 garlic cloves, minced
sea salt and black pepper, to taste

In a large bowl, combine all the ingredients for the pesto.

Add the courgette ribbons and tomatoes to the bowl and gently toss them through the pesto, being careful not to break up the vegetables.

Finish with a good grind of black pepper and serve.

My Tip
You can use many different variations of pesto, swapping in different herbs, bulking out with spinach and using different nuts. I particularly like to swap in walnuts as I think they work really well with the basil.

sides and salads

Pickled Fennel and Apple Salad

serves 2–4

This is a wonderful quick and easy salad with a really fresh vibrant flavour. I love to serve it with BBQ vegetables in the summer.

1 medium fennel bulb
1 Granny Smith apple, unpeeled

For the pickle juice
125ml rice wine vinegar
125g caster sugar
sprig of fresh thyme
6–8 Szechuan peppercorns

Place the rice wine vinegar, sugar, thyme and Szechuan peppercorns into a saucepan with 250ml water and bring to the boil; simmer until all the sugar has dissolved, about 3 minutes.

Using the slicing attachment on a food processor, or by hand, finely slice the fennel bulb (you might need to remove some tough outer leaves) and the unpeeled apple; I do this by working around the core.

Sieve the pickle juice into a jug to remove all of the bits and then add the sliced fennel and apple to it. Leave for about 5–10 minutes. I like the vegetables to be crispy and to have taken on the pickle flavour but you may prefer it pickled a little longer.

My Tip
I decorate this salad using the green leafy bits from the top of the fennel bulb.

vegetarian hassle free, **gluten free**

Braised Fennel with Roasted Orange Dressing

serves 4

I love fennel. I understand it's a vegetable that provokes very opposing views; however, this warm salad is rather a special way to spice up many a dish. For a vegetable-only main it's wonderful with a winter vegetable roast dinner, but I also like to serve it with salmon.

1 large fennel bulb, fronds removed (reserve for dressing), sliced into 1cm-thick slices
fresh thyme leaves, to serve
black pepper, to serve

For the dressing
1 large orange, zested and chopped into 8 pieces
1 cinnamon stick
2 star anise
10 black peppercorns
6–7 sprigs of fresh thyme
100g unsalted butter
1 tablespoon lemon juice
pinch of sea salt
○ *250ml–500ml vegetable stock, depending upon the size of your roasting dish*
drizzle of olive oil (if required, and to serve)

You will need
roasting dish or tin (I use a 30 x 18cm tin)

Preheat the oven to 180°C/160°C Fan/Gas Mark 4. Place the sliced fennel into a lightly oiled oven dish; it can fit quite tightly.

Scatter half of the orange zest, all of the chopped orange and all the other ingredients except the vegetable stock, olive oil and salt onto the roasting tin. Pour over the vegetable stock, so that it comes to the top of the fennel. (The amount of vegetable stock will depend on the size of your dish.)

Cook for approximately 30 minutes, until the fennel is caramelised and cooked through but still retains its shape.

Discard the cinnamon stick, star anise, black peppercorns and thyme sprigs. Drain the cooking juices from the dish; place them in a food processor or a stick blender and blitz to a smooth sauce. You may need to add a little olive oil to get a smooth purée-like consistency.

Place some of the purée onto a dish and arrange the fennel on top. Drizzle over some olive oil and sprinkle with fresh thyme and a little black pepper.

Asian-style Slaw

serves 6–8

Salads and coleslaws are wonderful additions to many dishes and I don't always want them heavy with mayonnaise. This is a lighter-style slaw, perfect with dishes like the Crispy Asian-style Pancakes (page 98) or BBQ Tempeh Bites (page 97) or just as a side with a lovely summer spread or BBQ. Like a lot of Asian-style dishes the ingredient list can look intimidating but once you have prepped it's the easiest thing to put together.

For the dressing
50ml sunflower oil
75ml rice wine vinegar
40ml golden syrup, honey or
  agave syrup
*2 tablespoons **gluten-free** soy sauce*
1–2 garlic cloves, finely minced
1 tablespoon Chilli Oil (page 212)
1 red chilli, finely sliced
juice and zest of 1 lime

For the vegetables
150g white cabbage, finely sliced
150g red cabbage, finely sliced
2–3 (150g) carrots, grated
75g onion, finely sliced
10g basil, chopped, stalks included
5g coriander, chopped, stalks
  included

To serve (just pick what you like,
  here are some suggestions)
toasted sesame seeds
unsalted peanuts, chopped
red chilli, sliced
basil, torn
coriander, chopped
spring onion, chopped

Combine all of the ingredients for the dressing and leave to marinate while you prepare the vegetables.

Place all the vegetables in a large bowl and combine well. Drizzle over the dressing and top with your chosen serving options, or just serve as is.

My Tip
This salad is really very easy to make and very versatile. If you keep to approximately 450g weight of vegetables you can add in red pepper, sliced Brussels sprouts, bean shoots, sugar snap peas or any other crispy vegetable that you want. I have just included the basic recipe for you to start off with but please make it your own. I prefer to use golden syrup or agave in recipes like this as I find honey too overpowering, but that's entirely your choice.

Hispi Cabbage with Garlic and Crème Fraîche Sauce

serves 4

We love cabbage at home but the children much prefer dark greens like kale or cavolo nero. However we all like this recipe, probably because it's full of garlic and crème fraîche, making it decidedly unhealthy – a very special delicious treat.

1 firm hispi cabbage
25g unsalted butter, plus
* 15g for frying*
splash of olive oil
1 shallot, finely sliced
2 garlic cloves
7g parsley, chopped
100g crème fraîche
sea salt and black pepper

Remove the loose outer leaves of the cabbage and trim off the end of the stalk, retaining as much of the cabbage as you can. Cut through the cabbage stalk into quarters.

Put the 25g butter and the splash of oil into a non-stick saucepan and place the cabbage quarters into the pan cut-side down. Cook for about 3 minutes, until golden. Turn over, place the lid on the pan and cook for another 3–4 minutes (depending on the size and density of the cabbage). Use a toothpick to test; you want the stalk to have a crunch to it but not be raw.

Remove the cabbage and put the 15g butter into the pan. Gently fry off the shallot for about 2 minutes, until softened. Add the garlic and chopped parsley and cook for a further 2 minutes, until softened. Be careful not to blacken the garlic and make it bitter.

Put in the crème fraîche into the pan with a good grind of black pepper and salt to taste, cook until liquid and bubbling and pour over the cabbage in the pan. (Alternatively, remove the cabbage from the pan, divide among four serving plates and pour the sauce over.)

Serve immediately.

My Tip
You can cook cabbage the normal way and then drain well. Make the sauce and toss through. You won't get the charred flavour but it will still be delicious.

........................the sweet stuff

Aquafaba
(Vegan Meringue)
Chocolate Mousse

serves 4

Whoever thought that using the water from a can of chickpeas could make lovely meringues? It's really one of the best cooking miracles that I have come across in the last of couple years. You can of course make traditional meringue and there are so many recipes on the internet to help you, but I thought I would include just a few of my favourite recipes for you to try at home using this miracle ingredient. When making chocolate mousse this way you are completely avoiding the whole issue of using raw egg white, so if you have any issues with that, or an egg allergy, this is a perfect solution for you.

○ *200g dark chocolate (or vegan chocolate), broken into small pieces*
pinch of sea salt (optional)
water from 1 x 400g can of chickpeas (the aquafaba); keep the chickpeas to make the Roasted Chickpea Snack with Paprika (page 22)
¼ teaspoon cream of tartar
2 tablespoons icing sugar

Place a bowl over a saucepan of boiling water so the bottom is not touching the water. Reduce to a simmer and place the chocolate in the bowl. Melt the chocolate, being careful not to overheat it so it goes grainy. For a salted chocolate flavour, add the pinch of salt and stir in. Once the chocolate is melted and very glossy, remove immediately from the heat and leave to one side.

Whisk the aquafaba until it forms stiff peaks. This will take a little longer than traditional meringue but persevere. You can test by holding the bowl over your head and if you don't end up with 'egg' on your face it's ready.

Sift in the cream of tartar and icing sugar and continue to whisk for another 2 minutes on high, until your meringue is lovely and glossy.

Add the aquafaba mix to the chocolate, one spoonful at a time, and fold in, using a figure-of-eight motion and keeping as much air as possible in the mixture so that it's light and fluffy. Repeat until all of the mixture is added to the chocolate.

I usually serve this in some stemless wine glasses, but you can serve it in whatever way you like. Once served, place in the fridge until you want to eat. This recipe can be made the day before you want to serve it.

My Tip
You can serve this simply as a mousse with whipped cream or coconut cream. However, I love to put some fresh berries or passion fruit in the bottom of a large wine glass and spoon the mousse over. You can grate on chocolate or add nuts. Or add flavourings into the mousse, like a few drops of peppermint or orange.

Clementine Cheesecake

serves 6

I'm not sure if this is exactly a cheesecake in that it's not quite traditional in method; but, whatever, I do love it and I don't know what else to call it. I wanted something light and citrussy to serve after a meal as a heavy pudding is not always right. We all enjoy it and hope you do too.

225g seedless clementines (or the little seedless easy peelers), washed but unpeeled
150g **gluten-free** Hobnobs or digestive biscuits
75g blanched almonds
75g unsalted butter, melted
100ml double cream
180g soft cream cheese
1 large egg
25g caster sugar
squeeze of lemon juice

You will need
20cm springform tin

Preheat the oven to 150°C/130°C Fan/Gas Mark 2.

Place the clementines in a saucepan of water, bring to the boil and simmer for 30 minutes, until the fruit is soft and tender. Drain and leave to cool completely.

Using a food processor or a rolling pin and a strong bag, crush the biscuits and almonds. Mix with the melted butter and line the spring-form tin with the crumb. Please go up the sides as well as the base and make sure there are no holes, as the filling is wet so it will leak. Place in the fridge until cold and set.

My Tip
You can prepare up until this point the day before you want to serve if necessary.

Remove the hard bit at the top of each clementine, then blitz thoroughly with the cream using a hand blender or food processor until you have a purée and all the big lumps have gone. A little texture is okay but no-one wants to eat a big lump of peel.

Whisk the cream cheese with the egg until there are no lumps, then add the sugar and continue whisking for a couple of minutes.

Add the fruit, with the squeeze of lemon juice, to the cream mixture; stir to combine and pour into your biscuit-lined tin. Place in the oven for 30–35 minutes, until the tart is set and slightly risen. Leave to cool. You can eat the cheesecake cold or at room temperature.

My Tip
I love the idea of using the whole fruit in this recipe, but please make sure there are no pips by buying seedless fruit or removing any pips before you blitz, as they will really upset the flavour of the cake.

Christmas Pudding with **Boozy Brandy Butter**

makes 1 x 2lb
pudding or 2 x
1lb puddings

I love Christmas pudding – not just on the big day, it's the whole event of making it, steaming it for the day and then setting it alight. It's a theatrical dessert; the day I make it, I go around all the people in the house getting them to stir the pudding and make a wish – they all think I'm mad but it's fun and just a great tradition. I know it's going a little out of fashion but I will continue to serve Christmas pudding, putting in my old sixpences and one £2 coin (which you don't have to give back) and enjoying the flaming finale to Christmas dinner. Apart from the cheese course which of course takes hours...

Day 1
30g candied peel
100g sultanas
100g raisins
100g currants
100g chopped glacé cherries
zest and juice of 1 lemon
*150ml good **gluten-free** beer (not lager, the darker the better)*
2 tablespoons black treacle
1 tablespoon mixed spice
½ teaspoon freshly grated nutmeg
½ tablespoon ground cinnamon
175g soft dark brown sugar
1 Granny Smith apple, grated (I don't bother to peel)
50ml brandy

Day 2
*100g **gluten-free** plain flour or chestnut flour*
150g ice-cold unsalted butter
2 large eggs
*75g **gluten-free** breadcrumbs (homemade is best or good shop-bought that are puffy and big, not like powder)*

Day 1
Place all the ingredients into a very large bowl and combine well. Cover with cling film and leave to one side for a day or two until you have the time for Day 2.

Day 2
Grease the tin(s) with butter.

Place 25g of the flour into a flat-bottomed bowl or plate (a pasta plate is perfect). Grate in a quarter (approximately 40g) of the butter, gently stirring it through the flour to coat, and then add to the Day 1 bowl and stir so that it's evenly spread through the mixture. Repeat this process three times, until all the butter and flour is evenly combined throughout the mixture.

Add the eggs and breadcrumbs and stir in well, until all mixed through.

Spoon the mixture in to your pudding basin and place into the steamer. I use a large-lidded saucepan and I have invested in some pudding basins that have handles and lids. Put two layers of greaseproof paper on the top of the puddings and cover with the basin lid. If you don't have a lid, make a lid of tin foil, then tie it tightly with string, passing the string around the bowl and over the top to make a cross so it acts like a handle.

Steam for 7 hours, making sure the water is topped up and does not boil dry. Then, remove from the steamer and uncover. Replace the

For the boozy brandy butter

150g unsalted butter
pinch of sea salt
50g icing sugar
50–75ml brandy, or to taste.

You will need

1 x 2lb steaming basin (or 2 x 1lb basins; see Tip)

greaseproof paper discs with fresh ones, replace the lid, and leave until the big day. (It will keep for months.)

Christmas Eve

To make the brandy butter, whip the butter, salt and icing sugar together until really light and airy and a light creamy colour. This will take a few minutes and you really do need to have a bit of patience to make sure it's perfect. It's much easier done with an electric hand whisk or stand mixer.

Once you are happy with the consistency of the whipped butter, slowly add in the brandy, continuing to whisk. Keep adding slowly being careful not to split the butter, until you are happy with the flavour. This can be kept in the fridge for up to a week.

Christmas Day

On Christmas morning put the pudding on to steam again for at least 2 hours and up to 4. Make sure it does not boil dry.

Serve the Christmas pudding with the brandy butter.

My Tips

This pudding makes a 2lb pudding but I find that a little big some years, so I make two 1lb puddings and keep one for the next year. I then do the same the following year so every year my pudding has been maturing for a whole year before we eat it. Reduce the steaming time to 5 hours for the initial steam and 2–3 hours on the day.

I don't feed my puddings as I marinade the fruit in lots of alcohol the day before.

I have found that as long as you stick to the weight of mixed fruit you can really mix it up. Add figs, more cherries, apricots, etc.; have a play and see what you prefer. You can add up to 40g of chopped nuts too, although that is not traditional in my house.

The brandy butter is brilliant paired with the Baked Apples Stuffed with Christmas Pudding (page 150), so make a big batch and use it across Christmas week.

Baked Apples Stuffed with Christmas Pudding

serves 6

I had almost forgotten about baked apples; my mum used to cook them regularly for pudding, but they had just fallen out of my cooking repertoire. Then last Christmas we had some Christmas pudding left over. I thought 'Why not try stuffing the apples with it?' and it was delicious. They are now firmly back in their rightful place and, come autumn, make a simple warming lovely dessert with custard or cream.

350g **gluten-free** *Christmas Pudding (or use homemade, page 146)*
100g blanched almonds, chopped
40g apricots, chopped
20g dried cranberries
juice of ½ lemon
2 tablespoons brandy
6 Bramley apples, of equal size, cored
50g unsalted butter, softened
6 tablespoons golden syrup

Preheat the oven to 200°C/180°C Fan/Gas Mark 6.

Place the Christmas pudding, almonds, apricot, dried cranberries, lemon juice and brandy into a bowl and gently stir to combine.

Meanwhile, wash and core the apples and place on a baking tray.

Place an equal amount of Christmas pudding mixture into each apple, and sprinkle any remaining mixture around the tray. Add a knob of butter and a spoonful of syrup to each apple. Put a little water in the bottom of the tray (to about 1cm) and place in the oven.

Bake for 50 minutes to 1 hour until the apples are soft but not collapsing.

Serve warm with the Boozy Brandy Butter (page 147), or with cream or ice cream, drizzled with the buttery juices and extra fruit.

My Tip
Baked apples can be stuffed with all sorts. I often use leftover mincemeat from making gluten-free mince pies. A mixture of dried fruits and golden syrup is delicious too.

Very Chocolately Cream Egg Cheesecake

serves 6

If I am honest, this is not my cup of tea. However, the men in my family seem to love it and it's a great one to do with children and real fun at birthday parties.

For the base
200g **gluten-free** digestive or
   Hobnob biscuits
100g unsalted butter
2 tablespoons cocoa powder

For the filling
360g cream cheese
75ml double cream
2 teaspoons vanilla bean paste
2 tablespoons caster sugar
1 tablespoon cocoa powder
○ 1 pack mini cream eggs, foil removed
○ 4 cream eggs, foil removed

You will need
loose-bottomed 7cm springform tin

Put the biscuits in a food processor and blitz until you have a smooth crumb. Alternatively put in a zipper lock bag and bash with a rolling pin. Melt the butter in the microwave or in a pan and add to the biscuit along with the cocoa powder. Mix thoroughly and then press into the bottom of the tin, working it up the sides and pushing down to make a crust. I use my hands for this as I find it easier. Chill in the fridge for at least 30 minutes, until set.

Mix the cream cheese, double cream, vanilla bean paste, sugar and cocoa powder in a large bowl and combine thoroughly. Chop up the mini cream eggs; reserve two for the topping and add the rest to the mixture. Cut the bigger eggs into half; reserve the best five halves for the topping, and add the remaining three halves to the mixture. Stir in well.

Put the cheesecake mixture into the chilled case and smooth the top. Gently press the five cream egg halves into the mixture and sprinkle round the remaining two chopped mini cream eggs.

Place in the fridge for an hour, then serve chilled.

My Tip
You could make these in little fairy cake cases and top with a mini cream egg rather than make a larger cheesecake.

Coconut Rice Pudding

serves 4–6

Rice pudding is one those truly comforting puddings. It's perfect if you are entertaining as you can leave it in the oven and it just takes care of itself. Serve this on its own or pair it with some lovely fruit, such as the Caramelised Pineapple and Rum (page 155) or the Ginger-spiced Mixed Berries (page 154).

coconut oil, for greasing
125g pudding rice
400g coconut cream (from a can)
400ml coconut milk (from a can)
50g caster sugar

You will need
20cm square oven dish with a lid (or a make a tight tin foil lid)

Preheat the oven to 150°C/130°C Fan/Gas Mark 2. Liberally grease the dish with coconut oil.

Put the pudding rice into your oven dish, add the coconut cream, coconut milk and sugar and stir well so that there are no lumps. The coconut cream and milk will separate in the tin so make sure you combine everything really well before cooking.

Put the lid or tight tin foil on the oven dish, and place in the oven for 2–2¼ hours until the rice is lovely and puffy and cooked through.

You can serve as is but if you want to add some fruit pineapple works particularly well and I always serve with cherries because they are my favourite. Otherwise the following pages offer some other suggestions.

My Tips
Don't be tempted to use a different rice: pudding rice will give you by far the best results in this dish.

If you are not going to eat straight away, you may need to heat some cream or coconut milk and stir it through before serving as this can go claggy if left too long.

Top to bottom: • • • • •
Ginger-spiced Mixed Berries
(page 154), Coconut Rice Pudding
(page 152) and Caramelised
Pineapple and Rum (page 155)

vegetarian hassle free, **gluten free**

Ginger-spiced Mixed Berries

serves 6

I know the combination of summer berries is not traditional, and you can leave the ginger out for a lovely result. However, I love ginger and genuinely think this is worth a try; it really works.

I like to try to use a whole packet of fruit when cooking so this will make more than you need to serve alongside the Coconut Rice Pudding (page 152), and it is wonderful spooned over the Breakfast Waffles (page 15), or with gluten-free pancakes.

450g mixed frozen berries
2 tablespoons caster sugar
50ml ginger wine
½ teaspoon ginger

Place all the ingredients in a pan and simmer slowly until all the fruit has defrosted and the sugar and ginger have dissolved. You want to keep the fruit whole if you can.

Serve warm with the Coconut Rice Pudding (page 152).

My Tip
I always use frozen fruit whenever I cook these berries unless we have a glut, for example when we go strawberry picking in the summer. They are so expensive to buy fresh and the frozen berries are so very good that you can't tell the difference once they are cooked.

Caramelised Pineapple and Rum

The combination of pineapple, rum and chilli makes this a really interesting and different dessert. It's perfect served with the Coconut Rice Pudding (page 152).

1 medium pineapple, peeled and cut into segments and the tough core removed

30g caster sugar

50g unsalted butter

50ml spiced rum, plus an extra splash to finish

1 red chilli, finely chopped (seeds and pith removed if you want milder flavour)

squeeze of lemon juice, to taste

25g macadamia nuts, chopped and lightly toasted, to serve (optional)

Place the pineapple, sugar, butter, rum and chilli in a pan with 50ml water and bring to the boil over a high heat. Reduce the heat to medium and continue to cook until the syrup is golden in colour, reduced by half and coats the back of a spoon. Leave to cool a little and add an extra splash of rum and squeeze of lemon juice to taste.

I think this is best served warm with a generous portion of the pineapple in a bowl and syrup poured over. You can sprinkle the toasted macadamia nuts for an extra special dessert, or serve it alongside the Coconut Rice Pudding (page 152).

My Tips

If you don't like alcohol just add in extra water; you will still have a lovely dessert that's suitable for everyone.

You can use canned pineapple and substitute the juice from the can for the liquid in the dessert if you wish. Be careful: it's softer and tends to break down more than the fresh pineapple.

Layered Pavlova with **Pears, Chocolate** and **Chestnut**

I have made this pavlova using aquafaba, the egg-free alternative. It really is a miracle ingredient. I don't think you can over-whip the way you can with eggs, but you need patience and a very good electric whisk or stand mixer as you need to whisk for much longer.

There are a few stages to this as it's a real centrepiece but it's well worth the effort. Feel free to fill with any of your favourite ingredients, but this is a more autumnal/ wintery take on the traditional pavlova – I often serve it at Christmas as an alternative to the heavier puddings. You could used canned pears, or even chocolate spread instead of the chestnut cream.

For the pavlova

water from 1 x 400g can of chickpeas (the aquafaba); keep the chickpeas to make the Roasted Chickpea Snack with Smoked Paprika (page 22)
1½ teaspoons cream of tartar
225g caster sugar

For the pears

3 Conference pears
250ml sweet sherry
100g sugar
1 cinnamon stick
4 star anise

For the chestnut cream

400ml double cream
2 tablespoons caster sugar
½ teaspoon vanilla bean paste
150g puréed chestnuts (from a can or vac pac is fine)

For the chocolate sauce

○ *50g dark chocolate*
100ml double cream

Preheat the oven to 150°C/130°C Fan/Gas Mark 2. Draw two 23cm circles (I draw round a cake tin) onto greaseproof paper and cut them out.

Drain the chickpea water and place into an electric mixer with the cream of tartar. Mix on high for about 10 minutes, until thick and glossy.

Add the sugar, a tablespoon at a time, to the meringue mixture, waiting until each is dissolved fully with no grains remaining before you add the next. I can hear the sound of the granules on my mixer blades but if you add the sugar slowly, allowing 5 minutes from start to finish, you should be safe. Make sure all the sugar is dissolved and the mixture is wonderfully thick and glossy.

Take a little of the mixture and dab it on the baking trays to hold the greaseproof circles in place. Then, using a spatula, spread half the mixture over each of the greaseproof paper circles.

Turn down the oven to 140°C/120°C Fan/Gas Mark 1. Place the meringue carefully in the oven and cook for 1 hour. Then turn the oven off and leave until completely cool. I like to leave it overnight, then assemble the pavlova the next day when needed.

Peel the pears, cut them in half and gently remove the cores using a teaspoon or melon baller. Remove the stems and the woody base and

Continued on page 158...

To garnish
chopped roasted hazelnuts (optional)

place the pears in a saucepan. Add the sherry, sugar, cinnamon and star anise and enough water to fully cover the pears, and simmer for about 10–12 minutes. The cooking time can vary quite dramatically depending on the ripeness and size of the pears, so check your pears regularly: they will be cooked when you can easily pierce them with a toothpick.

Remove the pears using a slotted spoon and place in a bowl. Bring the cooking liquid up to the boil and reduce until you have a lovely syrup that coats the back of the spoon. Pour the syrup over the pears and leave to cool completely. Again, the pears can be cooked the day before you assemble the pavlova.

To make the chestnut cream, put the cream, sugar and vanilla bean paste into a bowl and whisk until it forms soft peaks. Add the chestnut purée to the cream and whisk in quickly. Reserve for use.

To make the chocolate sauce, place a bowl over a saucepan of boiling water so the bottom is not touching the water. Reduce to a simmer and place the chocolate in the bowl. Melt the chocolate, being careful not to overheat it so it goes grainy. Once the chocolate is melted and very glossy, remove immediately from the heat and stir in the cream.

To assemble, place one of the meringue discs on a presentation plate and gently spoon or pipe half the chestnut cream evenly over it. (I find it easier to pipe the cream, as the meringue is very fragile.) Gently slice two of the pears; layer them on and drizzle half the chocolate sauce over them.

Carefully place the second disc of meringue on top. Cover with the remaining chestnut cream, add the remaining pears and chocolate sauce and sprinkle with the chopped roasted hazelnuts.

My Tip
I have found that aquafaba meringue is much more successful if cooked in layers or small meringues kisses rather than trying to make a larger meringue base, which always went a bit flat so this is my solution, layering it up.

Chocolate Swiss Roll with Grand Marnier Oranges

serves 6–8

This is a great recipe for when you want to do something a bit special. Please don't be put off by rolling the Swiss roll; it's really easy and if it's a bit wonky it tastes great so no-one should care. I have put in an optional unusual filling which is Christmassy but this tastes delicious filled with whipped cream and fruit if you prefer.

unsalted butter, for greasing
65g **gluten-free** plain flour
1 teaspoon **gluten-free** baking
    powder
15g cocoa powder, plus 1 tablespoon
    for powdering
½ teaspoon xanthan gum
4 large eggs
120g caster sugar

For the filling
300g double cream
30g icing sugar
1 tablespoon vanilla bean paste
2–3 tablespoons Grand Marnier
    (or whatever liquor you like)
zest of 1 orange

For the orange segments
2 oranges, whole, for segmenting
juice of 2 more oranges
4 tablespoons caster sugar
3 tablespoons Grand Marnier,
    plus a splash to finish

You will need
34 x 24 x 2cm Swiss roll tin

Preheat the oven to 200°C/180°C Fan/Gas Mark 6. Lightly grease the Swiss roll tin with butter and line with greaseproof paper.

Sift the flour, baking powder, the 15g cocoa powder and the xanthan gum into a bowl.

In a separate bowl, whisk the eggs and sugar really well for 3–5 minutes, until trebled in size and light and fluffy. Slowly add in the sifted flour mixture, a spoonful at a time, until it's all whisked in completely.

Gently pour the mixture into your lined Swiss roll tin and tip gently so that mixture goes into all the corners and is flat. Don't jolt it, you want to keep all that lovely air in your Swiss roll. Place in the oven for 10–12 minutes, until risen and cooked through; a skewer inserted into the centre should come away clean.

While the mixture is cooking, lay out a piece of greaseproof paper that is about 5cm bigger than your Swiss roll tin. Sift the remaining tablespoon of cocoa powder over the greaseproof paper.

Remove the Swiss roll from the oven. Gently tip it onto the cocoa-powdered greaseproof paper and take off the greaseproof paper that it was cooked in. Leave to cool for a couple of minutes, then gently roll into a tight cylinder using the greaseproof paper. Leave for a minute, then allow to unroll and cool.

While the Swiss roll is cooling, make the filling. Whisk the double cream, sugar and vanilla bean paste. Add in the Grand Marnier and orange zest and continue whipping until the mixture forms stiff peaks. Gently spread the filling onto the cooled Swiss roll and roll up again tightly.

Continued on page 160...

To segment your oranges, using a sharp knife carefully slice off the top and bottom of each orange. Using even downward strokes, slice the skin away from the flesh and discard. Remove any remaining white pith. Cut between the membranes to segment the orange; retaining any juices.

Put the orange juice, plus any juice retained from segmenting the oranges, into a pan with the sugar and the Grand Marnier. Bring to the boil and stir all the time until the sugar is dissolved and the juice thickens to a syrup that coats the back of the spoon.

Put the orange segments into the syrup and leave to absorb the flavours. For a stronger flavour, add a splash of Grand Marnier.

To serve, take a slice of the Swiss roll and drizzle over some of the syrup and orange segments.

My Tips
If you want a vanilla Swiss roll, replace the cocoa powder with 15g gluten-free plain flour.

If you prefer, you can use canned satsumas or tangerines instead of segmenting the oranges, and use a little juice from the tin for the syrup.

Baileys Bread and Butter Pudding

serves 6

My nanny and my mum have always served bread and butter pudding, with lots of double cream. It's not the healthiest and I used to giggle when they said it was to use up old bread. The cost of the cream and other ingredients far outweighed the waste of bread, but if you need that excuse to indulge in this delicious dessert then I am all in. This is a more indulgent version that I serve to guests who love sweet boozy desserts. The great thing is that you can put it together the day before, leave it in the fridge and then just pop it in the oven on the night.

500g **gluten-free** white bread loaf, liberally buttered and crusts cut off
75g white sugar
○ 75g milk chocolate chips
3 large eggs
250ml double cream
100ml milk
150ml Baileys Irish Cream

You will need
23 x 17cm tin or pie dish

My Tip
This pudding is a great way to use up left-over bread. Collect any left-over bread in a bag in the freezer, and once the bag is full you can defrost it and make the pudding.

Preheat the oven to 200°C/180°C Fan/Gas Mark 6.

Place a layer of buttered bread in the bottom of the dish and sprinkle with sugar and choc chips. Continue layering until all the bread is used in even layers. Reserve the top layer of sugar and choc chips.

Mix the eggs, double cream, milk and Baileys in a jug and pour over the bread, allowing it to be absorbed. It may not all get used at first; gently press the bread down with a spoon into the custard mix and leave to soak – you can add in the rest of the custard mix once it's absorbed.

If preparing in advance, cover and put into the fridge overnight to use the next day.

Sprinkle the top with the remaining sugar and choc chips and place in the oven for about 50 minutes, until risen and golden.

Remove from the oven and leave to cool for a little. The pudding is best served warm, with double cream.

Upside-down
Spiced Plum Cake

serves 6–8

This is one of my favourite recipes that I have churned out year after year for dinner and Sunday lunches. It's wonderful served during the autumn when we get a huge glut of plums, but I tend to make it all through the colder months as it's a real comfort pudding.

6 ripe red or purple plums
50g caster sugar
1 cinnamon stick
2 star anise
50ml brandy or dark rum (or water if you don't want to use alcohol)
1 orange

For the cake mix

175g unsalted butter, at room temperature
175g caster sugar
3 large eggs
175g **gluten-free** plain flour
½ teaspoon **gluten-free** baking powder
½ teaspoon xanthan gum
½ teaspoon mixed spice

To serve
○ Chantilly cream or custard

You will need
23cm springform tin

Preheat the oven to 180°C/160°C Fan/Gas Mark 4. Line the tin with greaseproof paper.

Cut the plums in half, working around the stone, then gently twist to separate. Remove the stone, using a teaspoon and trying to preserve the plum shape.

Put the sugar, cinnamon, star anise and brandy or rum into a saucepan with 200ml water. Using a vegetable peeler take about four large pieces of peel off the orange. Squeeze the juice out of the orange and add to the mix along with the pieces of peel. Bring to the boil, then reduce the heat to a simmer. Place the plums skin-side down into the syrup mix and gently poach for about 3–5 minutes (depending on how ripe the plums are). You want them to retain their shape but be tender when pierced with a toothpick.

Using a slotted spoon remove the plums, place them flesh-side down in the lined tin and leave to cool. Bring the syrup back up to the boil. It should be a lovely red colour from the plum skins. Then simmer for about 3–4 minutes, until it's reduced by two-thirds and slightly runnier than golden syrup. Turn off, leave to cool and set aside.

Whisk the butter and sugar until the mixture is light and creamy. Add the eggs one at a time, whisking all the time. If the mixture splits a little, add a tablespoon of the flour.

Combine the flour, baking powder, xanthan gum and mixed spice in a bowl, then sift into the creamed butter and sugar mixture in four separate batches, whisking all the time, until you have a lovely cake batter.

Gently spoon the cake mixture over the plums, making sure they are all covered with the mixture. Place in the oven for 25–27 minutes, until risen and golden. Remove from the oven, leave to cool and gently turn out onto a plate. To serve, strain over the syrup and add a large dollop of Chantilly cream or custard.

Chocolate
Whoopie Cakes

These are lovely cakes to bake with children as they are so easy – literally throw everything in and mix – and they are great fun. They can be made with a normal whisk but it's much easier if you have an electric one as the batter is quite firm.

75g unsalted butter, softened or melted
125g caster sugar
*150g **gluten-free** plain flour*
4 tablespoons cocoa powder
*2 teaspoons **gluten-free** baking powder*
2 large free-range eggs
1 teaspoon vanilla bean paste
½ teaspoon xanthan gum

For the filling (choose any of the following)
marshmallow fluff
chocolate fudge icing from a can
fresh whipped cream and fruit

Preheat the oven to 180°C/160°C Fan/Gas Mark 4. Line a baking tray with greaseproof paper.

Place all the ingredients into a big bowl and whisk them together well until you have a stiff batter.

Carefully place heaped tablespoons of the mixture onto the baking tray, about 3cm apart as they will spread. Try to make sure they are the same size as you want to sandwich them together and they need to cook evenly.

Place the baking tray in the oven (you can do this in batches) for about 8 minutes, until the cakes are cooked through and have crackles, but no moisture, on the top.

Remove from the oven and leave to cool, then carefully sandwich together using marshmallow fluff, chocolate fudge icing or fresh whipped cream and some fruit.

Banana and Hazelnut Loaf

makes 1 x 1lb
loaf (6–8 slices)

I could scream sometimes – my family go through stages, from always asking 'Where are the bananas? We've got no bananas!' to times when I fill the fruit bowl with bananas and then discover a bunch of brown bananas that none of them are ever going to eat. Hence the joy of banana bread. I particularly love this one, which uses dark treacle and hazelnuts. It's rich and delicious to eat.

125g unsalted butter, softened,
    plus extra for greasing
125g dark brown soft sugar
2 large eggs
125g **gluten-free** plain flour
1½ teaspoon **gluten-free** baking
    powder
¼ teaspoon xanthan gum
½ teaspoon cinnamon
1 teaspoon mixed spice
½ teaspoon sea salt
50g hazelnuts, roughly chopped
2 ripe bananas, roughly mashed
    with a fork
1 tablespoon black treacle

You will need
1lb loaf tin

Preheat the oven to 200°C/180°C/Gas Mark 6. Grease the tin with a little butter.

Cream the butter and dark brown sugar together until light and fluffy.

Add the eggs one at a time whisking all the time. If the mixture starts to split, add a spoonful of the flour. Keep whisking until the mixture resembles a mousse.

Combine the flour, baking powder, xanthan gum, cinnamon, mixed spice and salt in a large bowl, then sift into the creamed butter and sugar mixture in 3–4 batches and whisk in.

Gently stir in the chopped hazelnuts, bananas and black treacle until fully incorporated.

Spoon into the tin and smooth the top. Place in the oven and bake for 40– 45 minutes, until the loaf is risen and golden and a skewer inserted into the centre comes out clean.

Remove the loaf from the oven and leave to cool before removing from the tin. It can be eaten warm or cold.

My Tip
If you are not a fan of the spices I've used, feel free to add in your own; just stick to the quantities specified.

Coffee and Walnut Cake

serves 8

The only thing that I know I am allergic to is coffee. However ever since Rebecca took a sip of my mum's coffee as a young child, she has absolutely loved it. At about eight years old she asked me to make a coffee and walnut cake for her birthday cake; she had to stand next to me tasting the mixture as I made the cake! This cake is her absolute favourite and I can't change the recipe because I can't taste it. However, I am assured by all who do taste it that it's delicious, and if it works then that makes me happy. Whenever I make it I smile – it reminds me so much of her and having to make two cakes for her birthday because all her friends wanted a chocolate cake.

2 tablespoons espresso coffee powder
200g unsalted butter, at room temperature, plus extra for greasing
200g caster sugar
3 large eggs
*200g **gluten-free** plain flour*
*1½ teaspoons **gluten-free** baking powder*
½ teaspoon xanthan gum

For the icing
200g unsalted butter, at room temperature
125g icing sugar
1–2 teaspoons espresso coffee powder

To serve
75g walnuts (split into 2)

You will need
2 x 20cm sandwich tins

Preheat the oven to 200°C/180°C Fan/Gas Mark 6. Grease the tins with butter and line with greaseproof paper.

Mix the espresso coffee powder with 1 tablespoon cold water in a cup to form a smooth paste.

Whisk the butter and sugar together until the mixture is light and creamy. Add the eggs one at a time, whisking all the time until the mixture is soufflé-like in texture and really light and airy. If it starts to split, put a dessertspoonful of the flour into the mixture and continue to whisk.

Combine the flour, baking powder and xanthan gum in a bowl, then sift into the creamed butter and sugar mixture in four separate batches, whisking all the time. Add the espresso coffee mix and whisk in until it's all combined.

Divide the mixture between the sandwich tins. Place in the oven for 40–45 minutes, until the cake is risen and cooked all the way through and a skewer inserted into the middle of the cake comes away clean.

The icing can be made while the cake is baking, or can be prepared in advance and put in the fridge to use when ready.

Continued on page 168...

Whisk the butter until it's really light and fluffy, about 3 minutes. Sift in the icing sugar and whisk to combine. Mix the espresso coffee powder with 1 tablespoon cold water and whisk in.

My Tip

I find it easier to use the powdered espresso coffee. However, if you want to use the good stuff please do, but make sure it's cold first.

To serve, remove the cakes from the oven and leave to cool completely. Meanwhile, reserve some of the best walnut halves for decoration, and chop the rest. Pipe or spread half of the icing over the bottom half of the cake and sprinkle over the chopped walnuts, reserving some to decorate the top.

Put the top half back on the cake. Pipe or spread the remaining icing over the top and arrange the eight walnut halves around the edge and scatter the remaining chopped walnuts in the middle.

This cake will keep covered for up to 48 hours.

Christmas Cake

serves 12–16

My mum loves Christmas cake and so whenever I make it I cannot help but feel very happy as it's associated with such lovely memories. I used to try to cook mine in September and then feed it, however I have a cheat. I still cook it a couple of months in advance and wrap it well to decorate just before Christmas but I don't have to feed it all the time – I often forgot or just didn't find it very successful for getting that lovely smooth alcohol punch I associate with Christmas cake. Be warned – this is a boozy cake.

A week before baking day

250g currants
250g sultanas
150g raisins
250g glacé cherries, chopped
50g mixed peel
400ml brandy or dark rum

On baking day

*250g **gluten-free** plain flour*
½ teaspoon freshly ground nutmeg
1 teaspoon mixed spice
1½ teaspoons xanthan gum
pinch of sea salt
225g unsalted butter, softened,
*   plus extra for greasing*
225g dark brown soft sugar
4 large eggs
1 tablespoon black treacle

For the icing

1kg marzipan (you can buy ready-
*   made but there are plenty of recipes*
*   available)*
apricot jam, for spreading
○ *1kg royal icing, butter or fondant*
*   icing (you can buy ready-made*
*   but there are plenty of recipes*
*   available)*

A week before baking day, combine all the fruits and alcohol in a large bowl, stir well, cover tightly with cling film and leave in a corner in the kitchen out of the sun. Stir every couple of days to make sure the fruit has soaked up all the alcohol.

On baking day, preheat the oven to 150°C/130°C Fan/Gas Mark 2. Grease the tin with butter, or line it with greaseproof paper. Using the base of the tin, cut out two circles of greaseproof paper and make a hole the size of a 10p piece in the middle of each.

Sift the flour, nutmeg, mixed spice, xanthan gum and salt into a bowl.

Put the softened butter and sugar into a separate large bowl and whisk until light and fluffy; this will take a few minutes. Add the eggs one at a time, making sure they are really well whipped in, until the mixture is mousse-like and very light and airy. If it starts to split, add in a tablespoon of the flour mixture and continue to whisk. Repeat until all of the eggs have been whisked in.

Add about one-quarter of the flour mixture to the creamed egg and butter and whisk in thoroughly. Repeat until all of the flour is incorporated.

Put the fruit and black treacle in and carefully combine using a spoon and a figure-of-eight motion trying to keep as much air in the mixture as you can.

Spoon the mixture into your prepared tin and cover with the two circles of greaseproof paper.

You will need
23cm spring form tin

Place in the oven for 2 hours. Remove the greaseproof paper and continue cooking for another 45 minutes to 1 hour. Check with a skewer in the centre; if it comes cleanly away you know it's cooked.

Leave to cool completely, then wrap tightly in greaseproof paper and tin foil. This cake will keep for up to 3 months if wrapped properly. Place in a cupboard until a week before Christmas to take out and decorate.

To ice the cake you need to cover it in marzipan first. Warm enough apricot jam to coat the top and sides of the cake and brush all over so that the cake is sticky. Roll out your marzipan so that it will be big enough to cover the top and sides, making it as thick as you like (I go for about 1cm of marzipan all over), and cover the cake. Leave to dry for at least 2 days in a safe place (not where the dog can eat it).

Then ice and decorate your cake. I use royal icing but you can buy some lovely fondant icing and it really is up to personal preference. My daughter is a great artist so she models little Christmas themed figures for us but there are some beautiful ones to be bought.

My Tips
Please don't rush the first two steps on baking day. That's when we put the air into the cake and we need that in gluten-free baking.

I am not a fan of nuts in Christmas cake but I know a lot of people are. If you like, you can add in 25g of chopped almonds to the mixture at the same time as you add in the fruit.

St Clement's Cake

serves 8

I love citrus-flavoured things but so often I find that lemon or citrus cakes are just sweet without the tartness that I want from something labelled citrus. This cake certainly delivers on that and is definitely one of our family favourites.

250g unsalted butter, softened, plus
   extra for greasing
250g caster sugar
3 large eggs
250g **gluten-free** plain flour, sifted
2½ teaspoons **gluten-free** baking
   powder
½ teaspoon xanthan gum
zest and juice of 1 orange
zest and juice of 1 lemon

For the icing
200g unsalted butter, softened
75g icing sugar
zest of 1 orange, plus extra
   (optional) for decorating
zest and juice of 1 lemon
○ 2 tablespoons lemon curd

For the filling
○ 3–4 tablespoons lemon curd

You will need
23 x 7cm springform tin

Preheat the oven to 200°C/180°C Fan/Gas Mark 6. Grease the tin with butter and line with greaseproof paper.

Whisk the butter and sugar together until the mixture is light and creamy, about 3–5 minutes. This takes time but is well worth the effort. Add the eggs one at a time and keep whisking until the eggs are fully incorporated and the texture is almost mousse-like.

Combine the flour, baking powder and xanthan gum in a bowl, then sift into the creamed butter and sugar mixture in three batches, making sure each batch is completely mixed in before you put the next one in.

Add in the orange and lemon zest, beat in for another minute, then transfer into the lined baking tin. Smooth over the top and place in the oven.

Bake for 45–50 minutes, until the cake is risen and golden. Remove from the oven and allow to cool completely before icing.

To make the icing, beat the butter until almost white, for 3–5 minutes. Sift in the icing sugar. Add the zest of the orange, the zest and juice of the lemon and the lemon curd and whisk in.

Cut the cooled cake in half and spread the lemon curd filling over the bottom layer.

Spread about a third of the icing mixture onto the lemon curd and carefully place the top half of the cake on top. Spread another third of the icing mixture over the top of the cake and pipe the remaining third around the edges (or just spread all the remaining icing over the top).

Decorate with more zest of orange and lemon, if using, and serve.

...............doughs and pastry

Brazilian
Cheese Puffs

makes about 24

I love these little puffs of cheese. They are not difficult if you have a stand mixer or food processor or muscles like Arnie. I have tried to make them by hand; this is labour-intensive but achievable. The process is a little like making choux pastry.

250g tapioca flour
75ml milk
1½ tablespoons sunflower oil
½ teaspoon sea salt
a couple of splashes of tabasco
    (optional)
1 medium egg
100g vegetarian Italian hard
    cheese, finely grated, plus extra
    for sprinkling
60g ready grated mozzarella

Preheat the oven to 230°C/210°C Fan/Gas Mark 8. Line a large baking tray with greaseproof paper.

Attach a paddle blade to your stand mixer and place the tapioca flour into it.

Place the milk, sunflower oil, salt and tabasco, if using, into a saucepan with 100ml water and bring to the boil.

Pour the milk mixture over the tapioca flour and beat on medium until you have a breadcrumb mixture. If using a stand mixer you may need to stop and knead it a little to make sure all of the flour is incorporated from the bottom of the mixing bowl.

Add the egg and keep mixing on a medium speed until incorporated and you have a smooth dough that looks like fondant icing, shiny and smooth, which comes cleanly away from the bowl. Add the cheeses and continue to beat until all well combined.

Scoop out balls of dough (I use the tablespoon from my measuring spoon set to do this). Keeping your hands damp to handle the sticky dough, gently reshape the balls and place them on the baking tray, approximately 2cm apart.

Bake for 12–15 minutes, until the balls are be lovely and golden, and the inside is a stretchy dough with little holes (it should not be smooth and shiny). Sprinkle with the remaining cheese and serve warm.

My Tip
You can freeze the dough on the trays once balled, then take them out and cook them from frozen. You can also refrigerate the cooked puffs and just refresh with a couple of minutes' cooking in the oven to warm through.

Savoury Olive Crackers

makes 24
small crackers

Little tasty biscuits that I use mainly to go with cheese, these are easy to make and you can keep them in a sealed tin for up to a week, so they are perfect for special occasions.

200g **gluten-free** *plain flour*
50g unsalted butter, straight from the fridge, cubed
1 teaspoon xanthan gum
pinch of sea salt
good grind of black pepper
1 large egg
2 tablespoons olive oil
50g black olives, pitted and processed in a food processor until very finely crumbed

Preheat the oven to 220°C/200°C Fan/Gas Mark 7. Line a baking tray with greaseproof paper (or use a silicone mat).

Sift the flour and place in a bowl with the butter, xanthan gum, salt and pepper. Rub in using your fingertips until you have fine breadcrumbs.

Add the egg and combine into the mixture. Slowly add the olive oil until you achieve a smooth dough. (The exact amount of oil required will depend on the flour.)

Add in the olives and work through so that they are evenly distributed into the dough.

Roll out thinly onto a board; I use a 6cm cutter to cut out round biscuits, but you can cut square biscuits using a pizza cutter if you prefer. You will get slightly more crackers that way.

Place on the lined baking tray or silicone mat and bake in the oven for 20–25 minutes.

Leave to cool and place in a sealed box.

My Tip
You can sprinkle on seeds (we like sesame seeds) if you want to add another dimension to the cracker.

Crusty White Rolls

These almost didn't make the book. I was playing around with recipes earlier at home during our isolation period from Covid-19, making final edits to this book and I made up this recipe; I literally had a lightbulb moment. I felt it was too good not to include and tacked it on at the last minute to the publishers who luckily fitted it in. I hope you think it was worth it.

2 tablespoons granulated sugar or honey
*14g dried fast-acting **gluten-free** yeast*
175ml warm milk
*140g **gluten-free** plain flour*
*140g **gluten-free** brown rice flour*
140g tapioca flour
1 teaspoon xanthan gum
2 teaspoons sea salt (plus extra for sprinkling)
4g unsalted butter, warm, plus about 2 tablespoons for brushing on top of the rolls and a little extra for greasing
2 large eggs
½ tablespoon white wine or apple cider vinegar

You will need
18cm/7" springform sponge tin or cast-iron pot with a lid

Preheat the oven to 200°C/180°C Fan/Gas Mark 6. Lightly grease the sponge tin or pot with a little butter.

Add the sugar and yeast to the warm milk, stir and leave to stand in a warm place for about 15 minutes. It should form a head like a pint of beer; if it doesn't, your yeast may not be active so discard and start again.

Sift the flours, xanthan gum and salt into a large bowl and combine well. Make a well in the centre, and add in the butter, eggs, vinegar and active yeast mixture. Beat until you have a sticky dough.

Using lightly floured hands (or an ice cream scoop dipped in flour is perfect), roll six balls of dough weighing approximately 100g each and place them into your oiled tin. I put five balls of dough around the edge and one in the middle.

Put into a warm place and cover with a tea towel or lid. I leave mine on the top of the oven, towards the back, while it's preheating, for about 1 hour. The proving time will depend on how warm your place is so if the rolls need longer to rise it's not a problem. They should end up nice and puffy and touching each other but they won't double in size.

Brush with melted butter and sprinkle with salt and place in the oven for about 20 minutes, until golden.

These rolls are best served warm, but you can brush them with a little water and reheat in the oven for a few minutes if you are eating later.

Tiger Bread

makes 1 x
550g loaf

If I am honest, I struggled so much with this recipe. I made beautiful bread using one type of flour blend but as soon as I tested it with another brand it failed completely. It's a sad fact that there is no standard for flours in gluten-free cooking, so what works brilliantly with one brand fails with another. I could not in all consciousness publish a recipe that relied on something that most of us could not easily access. So, I went back to the drawing board and what I call base flours, and experimented for such a long time, determined only to use flours that we could access easily from health food stores or online. I am very proud of the result; this works very well and gives you a lovely tiger bread loaf. I hope you enjoy it as much as we do.

2 teaspoons granulated sugar
*14g dried fast-acting **gluten-free**
  yeast*
125ml warm water
125ml warm milk
*200g **gluten-free** brown rice flour*
100g cornflour
200g tapioca flour
*1 tablespoon **gluten-free** baking
  powder*
½ teaspoon xanthan gum
2 teaspoons sea salt
50g unsalted butter, softened
2 large eggs
*1 tablespoon white wine or
  cider vinegar*

You will need
2lb loaf tin

Preheat the oven to 180°C/160°C Fan/Gas Mark 4. Line the tin with greaseproof paper.

Add the sugar and yeast to the warm water and milk, stir and leave to stand in a warm place for about 10 minutes. It should form a head like a pint of beer; if it doesn't, your yeast may not be active so discard and start again.

In a separate bowl weigh out the brown rice flour, cornflour, tapioca flour, baking powder, xanthan gum and salt and combine well. I use a slow setting on my electric whisk to do this.

Place the butter, 1 of the eggs, the vinegar and the active yeast mixture into the bowl with the dry ingredients. Combine using a spoon and then your hands or use a dough hook/paddle. Keep kneading, mixing until you have a soft dough that comes away from the side of the bowl leaving no traces.

Gently shape into roughly the size of your tin then place into your prepared tin. Push gently into the tin and smooth off the top with your hand so that it's level.

Place in a warm place for 30–45 minutes; the bread will rise until it roughly doubles in height and cracks on the top, like tiger bread. The proving time will depend on the warmth of your proving place. I place mine on the top of the oven, towards the back, while it's preheating.

Beat the remaining egg and use it to egg wash the top of the bread (you can use a little melted butter if you prefer, see tip below).

Place in the oven and bake for about 45 minutes, until light golden and crusty on the top and a skewer inserted into the middle of the bread comes away clean.

Leave to cool a little before cutting. However, the loaf can be enjoyed slightly warm.

My Tips
I buy all of my flours online now with the exception of cornflour. You need to check they are gluten free but I have found they are easily sourced and no longer prohibitively expensive if you shop around.

Your loaf will be much more golden in colour when cooked if you egg wash but I was final testing recipes during the Covid-19 outbreak and I didn't want to waste an egg; I found brushing with a little melted butter as soon as your loaf comes out of the oven gives it a lovely shine and it still looks lovely. Egg wash or not is purely cosmetic and makes no difference to the taste.

French Bread

Decent bread is so hard to find and to make. This recipe is the most basic one I have been able to develop while still delivering a delicious crusty bread that we all crave. A French bread tin is essential to make this bread. I have a cheap and cheerful one that I found on the internet.

200ml milk
1 tablespoon lemon juice
2 teaspoons caster or
  granulated sugar
*14g dried fast-acting **gluten-free***
  yeast
*200g **gluten-free** plain flour*
*2 teaspoons **gluten-free** baking*
  powder
½ teaspoon bicarbonate of soda
1½ teaspoons sea salt
½ teaspoons xanthan gum
20g butter, melted (I use salted
  for flavour but up to you)

You will need
French bread tin

Preheat the oven to 200°C/180°C Fan/Gas Mark 6. Line the tin with greaseproof paper.

Combine the milk and lemon juice in a jug and leave to sit for 10 minutes, until it starts to form lumps and is sour. Warm the milk (I microwave it for 40 seconds) and add the sugar and yeast. Leave in a warm place for about 10–15 minutes. It should form a head like a pint of beer; if it doesn't, your yeast may not be active so discard and start again.

In a separate bowl sieve the flour, baking powder, bicarbonate of soda, salt and xanthan gum. Once the yeast mix has risen and is active put a well in the middle of the flour mixture and pour the yeast mixture in. Using a wooden spoon stir well to combine; the mixture will become instantly light and fluffy, so do not overwork.

Carefully spoon the mixture into the French bread tin, making sure it's level and leave 2–3cm at either end to allow the bread to rise.

Liberally brush over the melted butter and gently smooth down the dough to look like a loaf, so that it's shiny and even on the top. Don't push it down; just use the brush or your hands to smooth it.

Leave in a warm place to rise for 10 minutes, then place in the oven for 25–30 minutes, until golden and cooked through and a skewer inserted into the middle of the bread comes away clean. Remove and serve warm.

If the bread is wrapped well when it has cooled, it can be used the next day. Our favourite way to eat this, especially if it needs eating up, is as the Best Extra Cheesy Extra Garlicky Bread (page 48).

My Tip
Gluten-free dough is often much wetter than normal dough and this is a particularly fragile dough. You will see as you make it how instantly light and full of air it is. Don't over mix and just gently drop it into the French bread tin.

Tiger Bread (page 180), French Bread (page 183) and Flavoured Butters (page 213)

Scones

makes 6 scones

Are there many things better than a fresh scone from the oven covered in cream and strawberry jam? And yes, I do think that the jam should always go on first, and then lots and lots of cream, especially if you can get Cornish clotted cream.

350g **gluten-free** plain flour, plus extra for rolling out
2 teaspoons **gluten-free** baking powder
½ teaspoon xanthan gum
100g unsalted butter, straight from the fridge, cubed
50g caster sugar
1 large egg
150ml milk
1 large egg, beaten, to egg wash
100g sultanas (optional)

You will need
6cm pastry cutter

Preheat the oven to 180°C/160°C Fan/Gas Mark 4. Line a baking tray with greaseproof paper.

Sift the flour, baking powder and xanthan gum into a large bowl and combine well. Add the butter and rub between your fingertips until you have created a crumb.

Stir in the caster sugar and add the egg and milk. Use a spoon or your hands to bring the mixture together into a dough. Add the sultanas, if using. Continue to bring the dough together; you may need to add a little extra flour depending on the flour you are using. Add about 25g at a time until you have a slightly wet dough.

Turn out onto a well-floured board and, trying to work the dough as little as possible, use your hands to gently shape the dough and flatten it out to about 2cm thick.

My Tip
These scones are delicious but I find a lot of my most successful gluten-free bakes involve using fragile softer dough than you would usually expect. I flour my hands and just gently manipulate the dough; we don't need to work it but are trying to keep air in and keep the mixture fluffy.

Then flour your pastry cutter and cut out your scones. Drop them onto the lined baking tray or use a palette knife or spatula to transfer. When you have cut out as many as you can, fold your dough over, work it a little and cut out the rest, refolding the dough as you need to.

Egg wash and place in the oven for about 18 minutes. The scones are cooked when golden in colour and risen and a skewer inserted into the middle of them comes away clean.

Leave to cool before serving.

English Muffins

makes 4 muffins

Is it wrong to admit that when I was working on another recipe, I accidentally made the most gorgeous English muffins? Since then they have been a real favourite, particularly at the weekend when a late lazy brunch is just wonderful. I am sure some of the best recipes are the result of accidents – or maybe that's just my kitchen! These are lovely toasted to make Eggs Benedict and we really love them with Hampshire Fried Cauliflower with a Green Sriracha Salsa (page 31).

½ teaspoon sugar
7g dried fast-acting **gluten-free** yeast
125ml warm milk
100ml warm water
250g **gluten-free** plain flour
½ teaspoon **gluten-free** baking powder
¼ teaspoon xanthan gum
¼ teaspoon sea salt
splash of sunflower oil
knob of unsalted butter

You will need
9cm chef rings or pastry cutters, lightly buttered (optional)

Add the sugar and yeast to the warm milk and warm water, stir and leave to stand in a warm place for about 10 minutes. It should form a head like a pint of beer; if it doesn't, your yeast may not be active so discard and start again.

Sift the flour, baking powder, xanthan gum and salt into a large bowl and combine well, then beat into the live yeast mixture well until you have a thick batter.

Leave in the bowl in a warm place for 45 minutes to 1 hour. The dough will puff up and be really bubbly.

Put the splash of oil, and a tiny knob of butter for colour and flavour, into a large non-stick frying pan and melt the butter over a medium heat.

The muffins can be cooked using the chef's rings or pastry cutters to get an exact circular shape like the ones you see in the shops, but you can just drop the mixture in a tablespoon at a time and you will still get a lovely result, they just don't look as tidy.

Place the chefs rings, if using, into your pan and add 2 heaped tablespoons of the mixture to each, gently patting down to ensure that the mixture is evenly distributed. Cook over a medium heat for about 5 minutes, until lightly golden.

Use a spatula to turn the muffins over and gently remove the chefs rings. Cook on the second side for about 5 minutes or until golden; the muffins are cooked when their sides are not wet. Remove from the pan and leave to cool. These can be eaten warm or toasted like English muffins.

Fruit Bread

makes 1
small loaf

This is a rather lovely bread that you can toast or serve just with butter and jam. It's a very simple process once you have the ingredients weighed out and is well worth it.

1½ tablespoons caster sugar
7g dried fast-acting **gluten-free** yeast
125ml warm water
75g **gluten-free** brown rice flour
50g cornflour
60g tapioca flour
1 tablespoon **gluten-free** baking powder
1 teaspoon xanthan gum
1 tablespoon mixed spice
30g unsalted butter, softened, plus extra for greasing
1 large egg
50g caster sugar
25ml milk
½ tablespoon vanilla bean paste

For the fruit filling
100g sultanas
25g raisins
25g glacé cherries, chopped

You will need
900g/2lb loaf tin

Preheat the oven to 200°/180°C Fan/Gas Mark 6. Grease the tin with butter and line with greaseproof paper. Place the sultanas and raisins in a bowl and cover with hot water to allow the fruit to plump up.

Meanwhile, add the sugar and yeast to the warm water, stir and leave to stand in a warm place for about 10 minutes. It should form a head like a pint of beer; if it doesn't, your yeast may not be active so discard and start again.

Sift the flours, baking powder, xanthan gum and mixed spice into a separate bowl and combine well. I use my electric hand whisk on a low setting.

Put the butter, egg, caster sugar, milk and vanilla bean paste into a separate bowl and whisk to combine well. Add to the bowl of flours, continuing to whisk. Finally whisk in the active yeast mixture, until you have a wet dough. Cover and leave in a warm place for 15 minutes.

Drain the sultanas and raisins and leave to cool.

Once the dough has rested for 15 minutes, gently fold in the drained fruit and cherries and place in the prepared tin, smoothing to the sides. Drop the tin onto your worktop to make sure no large bubbles are trapped which might cause the bread to collapse. Place in a warm place in the kitchen for 30–40 minutes; the bread should rise to the top of the tin.

Sprinkle with sugar and place in the oven for 35–40 minutes, until a skewer inserted into the centre comes away clean. Leave the bread in the tin for at least 20 minutes to cool and turn out.

We love this served warm with butter and jam, but you can also keep it for 2–3 days in an airtight tin and toast it as you need.

My Tip
You can use any combination of fruit and nuts that you like; just keep to within 25g of the quantity stated.

vegetarian hassle free, **gluten free**

Sultana and Cinnamon Buns

makes 8 buns

Pastries are a huge favourite in our house. They are great on the move food, full of instant energy and easy to eat. These buns are packed full of flavour and I have found them to be a foolproof recipe as long as the yeast develops at the beginning. You can make them by hand, but I have to admit it's a lot easier with a kitchen mixer or food processor.

75g caster sugar
45g dried fast-acting **gluten-free** yeast
325ml warm water
450g **gluten-free** plain flour
50g cornflour
1 teaspoon xanthan gum
1½ teaspoons cinnamon
1 teaspoon fresh ground nutmeg
1 teaspoon sea salt
150g sultanas
75g unsalted butter, melted
2 large eggs

To finish
40g unsalted butter, melted, plus extra for greasing
extra **gluten-free** flour for dusting your hands
1 egg, beaten, to egg wash
40g demerara sugar
1 teaspoon cinnamon

Preheat the oven to 180°C/160°C Fan/Gas Mark 4. Liberally grease a baking tray with butter.

Add the sugar and yeast to the warm water, stir and leave to stand in a warm place for up to 15 minutes. It should form a head like a pint of beer and double in size; if it doesn't, your yeast may not be active so discard and start again.

Sift the flour, cornflour, xanthan gum, cinnamon, nutmeg and salt into a separate bowl and combine well. Toss the sultanas in a tablespoon of the flour mixture until coated, and reserve.

Once the yeast mix has developed, add it to the dry ingredients with the 75g melted butter and the eggs. Mix well, beating in either by hand or using a kitchen processor until a smooth dough is achieved. Add the sultanas and mix in until they are fully incorporated.

Divide your mixture into equal portions (I make eight buns with this mixture, each weighing about 130g). Flour your hands well, then gently roll each portion into a ball and place the balls on the baking tray about 2cm apart. Gently brush with the 40g of melted butter and then egg wash. You can smooth out rough surfaces at this time. Sprinkle with demerara sugar and a little cinnamon. Leave to prove in a warm place for 20 minutes, then place in the oven and bake for 25 minutes. Remove and leave to cool.

My Tips
I love these toasted for breakfast with lashings of butter and some marmalade.

To make these into hot cross buns you will need 50g cornflour mixed with about 3 tablespoons water. Add the water a tablespoon at a time until you have a paste. Place into piping bag with a small nozzle and pipe a cross on top of the buns. Once cooked, glaze with warm apricot jam and leave to cool.

Clockwise left to right: Chocolate Crackle Biscuits (page 190), Sultana and Cinnamon Buns (page 187), Fruit Bread (page 186) and Scones (page 184)

Chocolate Crackle Biscuits

makes about
20 biscuits

I think it's really important to get children cooking as soon as you can, with hands-on recipes, and baking is a great way to start that. These biscuits are lovely and easy to make and children can get their hands in, rolling them into balls. They are great for grown-ups too; we like to eat them when warm but they are great cold as well.

250g **gluten-free** plain flour
1 teaspoon **gluten-free** baking powder
50g cocoa powder
75g unsalted butter, softened
○ 50g chocolate chips
125g golden syrup
50ml milk
1 large egg
1 tablespoon vanilla bean paste
1 tablespoon cream cheese
pinch of sea salt
75g icing sugar

Preheat the oven to 180°C/160°C Fan/Gas Mark 4. Line two baking trays with greaseproof paper (or bake in batches depending on how many trays you have).

Sift the flour, baking powder and cocoa powder into a large bowl and stir to combine.

Add the butter, chocolate chips, golden syrup, milk, egg, vanilla bean paste, cream cheese and salt and using an electric whisk beat for about 3 minutes, until you have a smooth dough. It won't form a ball but will be more like a stiff cake mix.

Sift the icing sugar into a bowl.

Use a dessertspoon to measure out balls of dough about 30g–35g in weight, just a little smaller than a table tennis ball. The dough is sticky, so you need to drop the balls into the icing sugar and roll them in it. Once coated, place on the baking tray. You should have enough dough to make about 20 biscuits.

Put in the fridge for at least 30 minutes to chill the dough.

Place in the oven and bake for 15 minutes, they will be quite soft when you take out leave them to cool before eating.

My Tip
I have tried making this dough without chilling it, but I've come to the decision that it really is worth finding those extra 30 minutes for the final results. To weigh the biscuits, place your dish with the icing sugar on the scales – you can easily drop in the dough and weigh out your biscuits as you go.

Ginger Biscuits

makes about
20 biscuits

My very favourite biscuit is ginger and these are lovely – I have used them in the past to make gingerbread men for the children, with a lot of success. You can reduce the amount of ginger – I did when I was testing the recipes out for this book, but the family noticed and they were not impressed, so it's back in its full glory.

*250g **gluten-free** plain flour*
*¹⁄₂ teaspoon **gluten-free** baking powder*
*1 teaspoon **gluten-free** bicarbonate of soda*
¹⁄₂ teaspoon xanthan gum
¹⁄₂ teaspoon sea salt
¹⁄₂ teaspoon cinnamon
2¹⁄₂ teaspoon ground ginger
¹⁄₂ teaspoon mixed spice
125g unsalted butter, straight from the fridge, cubed
100ml golden syrup
1 tablespoon cream cheese

Preheat the oven to 180°C/160°C Fan/Gas Mark 4. Line two baking trays with greaseproof paper (or bake in batches depending on how many trays you have).

Sieve the flour, baking powder, bicarbonate of soda, xanthan gum, salt, cinnamon, ground ginger and mixed spice into a bowl. Using your fingertips rub in the cold butter until you have created a crumb.

Add in the golden syrup and, using a wooden spoon, combine to form a soft dough.

Wrap in cling film and chill in the fridge for at least 30 minutes.

Lightly flour a board and rolling pin and roll out the dough to about 0.5cm thickness. Cut out your biscuits, using a 6cm cutter (I use the flat side, not the crinkly one). When you have cut out as many as you can, reroll the dough and cut out more biscuits; you should get about 20. Place the biscuits on the baking trays, about 1cm apart.

Place in the oven for 10–12 minutes, until slightly golden.

Remove from the oven and leave to cool. The biscuits will take a while to set once out of the oven.

American-style Chocolate Chip Cookies

makes around
30 cookies

Surely everyone loves a biscuit! Even if, like me, you are not a dunker these American-style choc chip cookies are wonderful, especially if eaten when warm – such a different experience to our crunchy biscuits. Please feel free to add in nuts or a mixture of chocolate or some fruit if you want.

These are fab eaten cold but best when they are warm. If you cook these when anyone else is in the house, they will be eaten immediately. My kids love to sandwich them with ice cream as a special treat.

*500g **gluten-free** plain flour*
1 teaspoon xanthan gum
½ teaspoon sea salt
½ teaspoon bicarbonate of soda
*1 teaspoon **gluten-free** baking powder*
300g caster sugar
○ *350g milk chocolate chips*
150g unsalted butter, at room temperature
2 large eggs
1 tablespoon pure vanilla extract

Preheat the oven to 180°C/160°C/Gas Mark 4. Line two or three baking trays with greaseproof paper (or bake in batches depending on how many trays you have).

Place the flour, xanthan gum, salt, bicarbonate of soda, baking powder and sugar in a large bowl, and stir to combine.

Place about 300g of the chocolate chips in a small bowl. Add about 1 teaspoon of the dry ingredients, toss to coat the chips and set aside.

Add the butter to the rest of the dry ingredients and stir until the mixture is the texture of breadcrumbs. Add the eggs and vanilla and mix to form a soft stiff dough. Add the chocolate chips and mix until well combined.

Divide the cookie dough into about 30 portions (about 50g each). Flour your hands well, then gently roll each portion tightly into a ball and press it into a disc approximately 1cm thick and 8cm round. Place the balls on the baking trays about 2cm apart, sprinkling a few more chocolate chips onto each ball as you roll and pressing it gently on the top.

Bake for 10 minutes; the cookies will look a little underdone but will firm up within 5 minutes. Remove from the oven and allow the cookies to cool on the baking trays for about 5 minutes or until firm before transferring to a wire rack to cool completely.

My Tip
This mixture makes around 30 cookies, which is a lot. I bake half, then roll the remaining mixture into balls and lay them gently into a freezer bag and freeze so the balls don't touch. You can then take as many as you need out of the freezer, defrost and bake them when required.

Shortbread Biscuits

Who doesn't love shortbread? It's just a wonderful comforting biscuit, a real favourite with a cup of tea. This is a really lovely recipe, easy to put together, and a great one to do with the children if they like baking. This recipe is linked with my Drop Biscuits (page 195), because I usually use half the mixture for the shortbread (as eight shortbread biscuits are enough for us), then make the drop biscuits with the other half of the mixture.

175g unsalted butter, softened, plus
 extra for greasing
100g caster sugar
300g **gluten-free** brown rice flour
¼ teaspoon **gluten-free** baking
 powder
½ teaspoon xanthan gum

Preheat the oven to 190°C/170°C/Gas Mark 5. Line a baking tray with greaseproof paper.

Place all the ingredients in a bowl and combine, using your fingertips, until you have a dough. It will feel crumbly and dry.

Transfer the mixture to your baking tray and press it down into the tray, making the top as smooth as possible.

Place in the oven for 25–30 minutes, until just very lightly golden and the biscuit is set.

Remove from the oven and cut into 8–12 segments but leave in the tray to cool.

You can keep these shortbread biscuits in an airtight tin for 3–4 days.

My Tip
If you want a bit of extra luxury, dip in melted chocolate. Ben adds gluten-free sprinkles – Ben will add sprinkles to anything!

Drop Biscuits

makes 8–10

I often make the Shortbread Biscuits mixture (page 194) but only want eight shortbread biscuits; so I combine that bake with these quick cookies, using half the shortbread mixture for each.

a half quantity of Shortbread Biscuits mixture (page 194)
1 large egg
○ *100g milk or dark chocolate chips or sultanas*
granulated sugar, to sprinkle

Preheat the oven to 200°C/180°C Fan/Gas Mark 6. Line a baking tray with greaseproof paper.

Mix the egg into the shortbread mixture along with the chocolate chips or sultanas.

Scoop spoonfuls of the mixture onto a baking tray about 3cm apart (I use the tablespoon measure from my measuring spoons to do this). There is no need to shape them, but sprinkle them lightly with granulated sugar.

Place in the oven for 8–10 minutes, until golden and slightly brown around the edges. Remove from the oven, leave to cool and eat.

My Tip
You can use fruit and nuts in these. We have made them with dried cherries or raisins and nuts, which work really well.

Rough Puff and Flaky Pastry

makes approx.
600g pastry

I know you can buy ready-made gluten-free puff pastry but if you take the time to make it yourself it really does gives wonderful results. As with all baking a little love and patience goes a long way with this recipe. I know vodka is an unusual addition, but the theory is that as the pastry cooks the alcohol evaporates, making the pastry beautifully flaky. Having tested it, I believe it works and you have no alcohol in the final result. However, if you don't want to use vodka, ice-cold water is fine.

Step 1
50g cornflour
100g **gluten-free** white rice flour
150g **gluten-free** plain flour, plus
   extra for sprinkling
1½ teaspoons xanthan gum
1 teaspoon sea salt
125g block of unsalted butter, frozen
1 large egg
2 tablespoons vodka
5–6 tablespoons ice-cold water

Step 2
50g **gluten-free** plain flour
50g **gluten-free** white rice flour
200g unsalted butter, frozen
1 large egg, beaten, to egg wash

My Tips

Quite often with gluten-free baking you can ignore a lot of the traditional tips, as we don't have to wait for gluten to react in breads etc. However, when making the puff pastry please keep everything as cold as possible, including bowls and other equipment. It really will make a difference; in fact if you can't grate the butter the recipe becomes unworkable.

When I weigh out the butter before freezing, I add an extra 15g; as you can't grate to the end of the butter, this gives you a bit extra to hold onto. I freeze the butter overnight and run it through the largest setting of the food processor to grate. Keep it in the fridge between rolling out.

Preheat the oven to 220°C/200°C Fan/Gas Mark 7.

Step 1

Place the cornflour, rice flour, plain flour, xanthan gum and salt in a large bowl and stir to combine.

Remove the 125g block of butter from the freezer. Making sure the end is still wrapped in paper so your hands don't melt it, and using a large grating side, grate about a fifth of the butter into the flour mixture. Using a tablespoon, stir the grated butter gently into the flour, so that all the individual bits of butter are coated in the flour. You will need to gently shake and scrape the inside of the grater after each go and combine that too. Continue this process until all the butter is combined into the flour.

Add the egg and vodka and 1 tablespoon ice-cold water and gently stir in. Continue to add ice-cold water, a tablespoon at a time, and using your hands gently knead the mixture until it starts to come together into a ball of dough and comes cleanly away from the sides of the bowl. The exact quantity of water will depend on the flour you are using and even the room temperature, so go slowly as you add the water and take your time.

The pastry should be marbled with butter, and soft and pliable. Don't be tempted to overwork it. Sprinkle with a little plain flour and then gently wrap in cling film. Place in the fridge for 30 minutes.

You could use the pastry at this stage, just flour a board and roll it out as needed, but it's even flakier if you follow the next step.

Step 2
Combine the plain and rice flour well and liberally dust a surface using the combined flour.

Remove the dough from the cling film. Place on the floured surface and roll out, dusting liberally with flour to stop it from sticking, until the pastry measures approximately 30 x 25cm. The first stages of rolling need more work so, as you go, push in ragged edges with your hands and work the pastry into a nice even rectangle shape.

Take the 200g butter out of the freezer and grate a fine layer of butter over approximately half of your dough. You will need about 25g (an eighth) of the butter (it's not exact – just use your eye).

Fold the dough from the top to the bottom, creating an envelope for the butter. Turn the dough 90 degrees and roll out again to 30 x 25cm. Dust with more flour (it is important to do this between layers to get a true flaky pastry), and repeat until all of the butter is used up. I usually use about 75g of the plain flour I weighed out. You will notice the pastry begin to look and feel like it should and be marbled with butter. That's as it should be.

Once you have used the last of the butter you can use the pastry straight away, however I find it best to fold it into a block and place in the fridge for at least 30 minutes. You can also wrap in cling film and freeze it.

When you want to use the pastry, roll out as usual to the depth of a 10p piece. I always egg wash pastry – if you want a very professional finish just use the egg yolk for that very shiny golden finish.

Bake the pastry for about 15–20 minutes depending on what you are using it for. It should be risen and golden and beautifully flaky.

Shortcrust Pastry

makes 500g

This is my classic shortcrust pastry recipe which I use for everything and was published in my first book. Adding the water at the end is key: too much and the pastry will be sticky and hard, too little and it will be crumbly, so take your time with that last tablespoon.

Gluten-free pastry will not colour in the same way as regular pastry will, so be sure not to overcook it. Egg washing before cooking will help achieve colour too.

50g cornflour
*250g **gluten-free** plain flour*
1 teaspoon xanthan gum
pinch of sea salt
125g butter, straight from the fridge, cubed
1 large egg

Put the cornflour, flour, xanthan gum and salt in a large bowl with the cubed butter. Gently rub the butter into the flour using your fingertips until you have created a crumb.

Make a well in the centre and add the egg and 2 tablespoons cold water. Use your fingers to stir the mixture and incorporate the egg and water. If it's still a little crumbly, add a little more water and gently bring the pastry dough together with your hand, kneading lightly until it forms a ball and comes away easily from the sides of the bowl.

My Tips
I use the pastry straight after making it; if you refrigerate it for too long, it will become hard and unusable.

I roll it between two sheets of greaseproof paper as it's stickier than usual. To use, I take the top sheet of paper off and just pick up the bottom sheet with the pastry on it and place it carefully into the tin, then I remove the other sheet. If the pastry tears, don't worry, it's so much easier to patch than regular pastry. Even if you have some small cracks in the pastry after blind baking, you can patch these with a little raw pastry.

Finally, I have found many differences depending on which flour I use. This recipe is my standard, but some flours need a little more or less water. The more water, the harder the pastry, so it's a careful balance!

Sweet Shortcrust Pastry
Add 2 teaspoons icing sugar instead of the salt.

Cheese Shortcrust Pastry
Add 50g finely grated vegetarian Italian hard cheese to the dough after it's come together, and work it through.

Perfect Gluten-free Pasta

makes about
750–800g
pasta dough,
enough to feed 6

I am so very proud of this recipe. Pasta is something that is really at the core of most of our diets today and Ben loves it. While the dried pastas on the market have come on leaps and bounds, to be honest, there is nothing like a bowl of freshly made pasta. This recipe comes from a long time of trying, leaving it alone and trying again to get the best pasta I could without too much fuss. You can roll it out and cut it to make tagliatelle and lasagne sheets but if you have a pasta maker it will make your life so much easier. Likewise, you can mix it by hand but a mixer with a dough hook helps speed the process along.

The amount of egg in this recipe seems like a lot, but please trust me, the recipe does work and needs it for flavour and texture. You can buy liquid egg and measure out the correct quantity which would be 64g per egg, 384g in total.

*375g **gluten-free** plain flour,*
plus 75g extra for kneading
and dusting
*125g **gluten-free** brown rice flour*
1 teaspoon sea salt
2½ teaspoons xanthan gum
6 extra-large eggs

Place all the dry ingredients in a bowl and stir to combine well. Make a well in the centre and add your eggs. If using a mixer with a dough hook attached, put onto a low speed for about 3 minutes, until you have a ball of dough that leaves the sides of the bowl clean. If mixing by hand, use a fork to gently work in from the middle to the outside, slowly incorporating the flour and the egg. Towards the end you will need to get your hands into the dough, gently kneading to bring it together.

Once you have a ball of dough, flour a board or worktop with about 25g of plain flour and place the dough on top. Start gently kneading to bring it together; you might need to add a little more flour but keep kneading until it's no longer sticky but a nice smooth dough with a bit of a shine. You might need to add more flour when rolling out, but this depends on the make of flour you are using.

Split the dough into 12 and cover with a clean towel or cling film to stop it drying out while you work. Working with one piece at a time, gently roll each one into a long rectangular-like shape.

If you are hand rolling using a rolling pin, roll until as thin as required, gently flour and cut into strips of the required width for lasagne or tagliatelle, depending on what you are making.

Continued on page 201...

doughs and pastry

If using a pasta maker, make sure you have plenty of flour to hand, as well as a couple of clean tea towels to keep the dough covered at each stage. The process requires a bit of patience as different flours react differently, so you may find you need to coat your dough in a little more flour to get it to run through the pasta maker smoothly.

Run the dough through the number 1 setting of the pasta roller a couple of times. (If you find it breaks, roll it back into a ball, coat in a little more flour and try again.) I try and keep my dough to a maximum length of 30cm to ensure it's easy to work with, and any longer runs a risk of breaking. Lay the strip of dough on the floured worktop, cover with a tea towel and repeat the process with the rest of the dough, until all have gone through the number 1 setting.

Dust the sheets of dough in more flour and run the dough through the machine on the number 2 setting. Repeat the process for the number 3 setting, again dusting with more flour to stop the dough sticking. I usually stop at the number 3 setting, but if you want spaghetti then run through on the number 4 setting.

Change the setting to cut your pasta noodles, and run the sheet of dough through one final time with a shallow dish underneath to catch the pasta as it falls. Toss with flour to stop them sticking. If not cooking immediately, cover lightly with a cloth and leave in a cool place, but it does need to be cooked the same day you make it.

To cook, place a large pot of water, heavily salted, onto the stove to bring to a ferocious boil. Carefully drop the pasta into the water and cook for about 2 minutes; it should rise to the top. The exact amount of cooking time will depend on how thick your pasta is, but it should be a little al dente. Drain and use as you would ordinary pasta. I have included a couple of my favourite sauces for you in the dinner chapter.

My Tips

Making pasta for the first time is always a little daunting but once mastered the results are wonderful and make such a difference to your final dish. Trust your instinct and go slowly. You will feel when the pasta dough is right, it won't feel sticky but should feel smooth and not bumpy at all.

I use Shipton Mill gluten-free plain flour in this recipe. Gluten-free flours differ so much but please try to avoid any that are really chalky and white. For a lot of recipes you can get away with these, but this recipe really needs a good flour.

dress it up

Spicy BBQ Sauce

makes 450ml

BBQ Sauce is a wonderful thing and we love it. This is an easy sauce to put together and it really works. You can keep it in the fridge and use it for whatever takes your fancy.

200ml white wine vinegar
100g tomato paste
100ml honey or golden syrup
50ml olive oil
2 large garlic cloves, minced or
  finely grated
1 tablespoon hot smoked paprika
1 tablespoon dried mixed herbs
1 tablespoon dried chipotle flakes
1 teaspoon sea salt
1/2 teaspoon ground black pepper

Combine all the ingredients. The sauce will keep in the fridge in a sealed jar for a week.

My Tip
If you do this for a special recipe, hide it. I have known my children dip everything in it, from garlic bread to crisps, and use it all before I get a chance to.

vegetarian hassle free, **gluten free**

Sweet and Sour Sauce

makes approx. 400ml

Sweet and sour sauce is my husband's favourite, and one of Ben's too, so to be able to make a quick easy gluten-free version was a must from the very start of our family's venture into gluten-free cooking. I hope you like it as much as we do.

2 tablespoons **gluten-free** *soy sauce*
2 tablespoons runny honey or syrup
○ *2 tablespoons tomato ketchup*
2 tablespoons white wine vinegar
½ x 435g can of pineapple, chopped into chunks and juice reserved
sunflower oil, for frying
1 bunch of spring onions (about 400g) finely chopped
1 garlic clove, finely chopped or minced
1 mild red chilli, deseeded and finely chopped
½ red pepper, chopped into chunks
½ green pepper, chopped into chunks

In a small bowl, combine the soy sauce, honey or syrup, tomato ketchup, white wine vinegar and 2 tablespoons of the pineapple juice from the can, and reserve.

Splash some oil into a wok or good non-stick frying pan and heat until smoking hot. Add the chopped spring onions (reserving some of the green bits on the top for serving) and stir, then cook for approximately 2 minutes, until just starting to brown. Add the garlic, chilli and peppers and cook for a further couple of minutes.

Add the sauce, stir and leave to bubble for 3–5 minutes; it will go a little darker and thicken into a syrupy consistency.

This sauce goes beautifully with the Sweet and Sour Crispy Tempeh recipe (page 61), and will keep for 3–4 days in a sealed container in the fridge.

205

dress it up

Satay Sauce

makes approx.
250ml

Drizzle this over salads, crispy tofu, tempeh or any vegetables. It really is delicious. I often make it the day before and keep it in the fridge to use as needed.

2 teaspoons sunflower oil
½ teaspoon powdered ginger
2 garlic cloves, finely minced
○ *175g crunchy peanut butter*
*2 tablespoons **gluten-free** soy sauce*
2 teaspoons lime juice
○ *½ tablespoon sriracha (or to taste)*
2 teaspoons golden syrup

Combine all the ingredients in a large bowl and stir well. Add about 75ml hot water until you have the consistency you require.

The sauce will keep in the fridge for 2–3 days.

My Tip
You can use other nut butters to make this satay. I love the traditional crunchy flavour of peanut butter. I find some of the others can seem a lot oilier and more bitter, so you may need to adjust oil and syrup quantities a little.

Sriracha Mayo
Corn Salsa

serves 4–6

This takes less than 10 minutes to cook. It goes brilliantly with grilled or BBQ vegetables but we particularly love it with the Black Bean Burgers (page 100).

2 tablespoons olive oil
250g frozen supersweet sweetcorn
1 red chilli, chopped
1 red onion, chopped
juice of 1 lime
½ teaspoon sea salt
10g coriander or flat-leaf parsley, chopped
○ *3 tablespoons mayonnaise*
○ *1 tablespoon sriracha (or to taste)*

Put the olive oil, sweetcorn, chilli and red onion into a saucepan and cook over a low heat, stirring until the sweetcorn is defrosted and cooked through but still remains crunchy.

Put into a bowl to cool while you prepare the other ingredients.

Once cool add in the lime juice, salt, chopped coriander or parsley, mayonnaise and sriracha. Stir together and serve.

The salsa will keep in the fridge for 1–2 days.

My Tip
You can char the sweetcorn beforehand for extra flavour, as in the recipe for Elotes-style Corn (page 101). If you do this, then just gently warm the onion and chilli together in olive oil to bring out the flavours for about a minute before combining.

Rich Tomato and Olive Sauce

serves 6–8

This sauce is based on the first ever dish I served on *MasterChef*. I remember John Torode telling me he wasn't just tasting; he was eating because it was so delicious and I was fast-tracked straight into the second round. This is a slightly lighter version. It pairs beautifully with the Broccoli Roasted with Lemon and Pine Nuts (page 123).

1 garlic bulb
splash of olive oil
3 medium carrots, cut into
  chunky slices
1 medium onion, peeled and
  roughly chopped
3–4 celery stalks, chopped
1 leek, chopped
250ml Sauvignon Blanc wine
○ *1 litre vegetable stock*
250g tomato passata
2 bay leaves (fresh if possible)
4–5 sprigs of fresh thyme
10–12 stoned Kalamata olives
  from a jar
250ml brine from the olive jar
a few chopped black Kalamata
  olives, to serve (optional)

Cut the garlic bulb in half. Place both halves in a large saucepan with the oil, carrot, onion, celery and leek and fry them over a low heat for about 10 minutes. You want the mixture to be a lovely golden brown and really starting to caramelise. Stir to make sure the vegetables are evenly cooked.

Turn up the heat and add in the wine, bring to the boil, turn down the heat to a simmer and reduce the wine for about 5–7 minutes, until you have barely a tablespoon of wine left and you are scraping all the lovely golden bits off the bottom of the pan.

Add in the vegetable stock, passata, bay leaves, thyme, olives and brine.

Bring back to a simmer and reduce the mixture by two-thirds; this will take about 30–40 minutes. You will end up with a beautiful, luxurious orange red sauce. You can chop in some Kalamata olives to finish if you want.

This sauce can be frozen if you have too much, otherwise it keeps in the fridge for 3–4 days in a sealed container.

My Tip
I use a flat-bottomed wooden spoon whenever I make sauces. It works brilliantly well for scraping off all the lovely golden tasty bits of flavour that you want in order to make your sauce really wow.

Chilli-spiced Roast Tomato and Red Pepper Dip

serves 4–6

This is a lovely dip that I have made to mimic one served at Harry's favourite chicken restaurant. It's great to serve with lots of things but we love it with the Mozzarella Sticks (page 25). It's very quick to do and you can keep it in the fridge for 3–4 days in a covered dish. It can be served warm or cold.

209

200g cherry tomatoes
splash of olive oil
1 tablespoon chilli oil
1 small red onion, chopped
2 garlic cloves, skins left on
1½ tablespoons mixed dried herbs
1 red pepper, deseeded and chopped

To finish
50ml olive oil
Chilli Oil (page 212), to taste (or use smoked oil for deeper flavour)
sea salt

Preheat the oven 180°C/160°C Fan/Gas Mark 4.

Put all the ingredients (except the oils and salt to finish) onto a roasting tray and toss to coat in the oil.

Place in the oven for about 20–25 minutes, until the vegetables are charred. Remove from the oven, leave to cool and remove the garlic cloves from their skins.

Blend all the ingredients and the oil from the pan together with the 50g olive oil, until smooth and red. You can leave some lumps – it's not a purée. Add chilli oil and sea salt to taste, and serve or store as above.

My Tip
Try to get a lovely char on the vegetables for added flavour.

dress it up

Vegan Cheese Sauce

makes about
600ml

So many friends are vegan or dairy free now and professionally I never get asked to design a menu without a vegan option. So I thought it only fair to put some of my simple recipes that I have compiled over the years into this book. They really make my life easier when preparing meals or menus for all. This simple one-step cheese sauce is a favourite as it's very easy to put together and versatile in use.

2 x 350g packs silken tofu
2 tablespoons lemon juice
3 tablespoons olive oil
1 tablespoon garlic salt
○ *1–2 teaspoons yeast extract*

Place all the ingredients in a food processor and blend until smooth and lump free. It will be the texture and thickness of a cream cheese. Alternatively, use a stick blender.

My Tip
I use this cheese sauce as a replacement in many different recipes and with many add-ins (the spinach in the Vegan Lasagne on page 92 for instance). It's very versatile and so easy. It will keep in the fridge, covered, for up to 48 hours.

Great Veggie Stock
and **Veggie Gravy**

makes approx.
1 litre of stock

A huge thank you to my daughter Rebecca for this. She makes fabulous vegetable gravy which we freeze in portions and defrost as needed. The base of the gravy is a delicious stock, which can be used for any recipe that requires veggie stock, or made into this gravy.

I know this uses vegetable stock cubes, but I am more than happy to cheat a little if you end up with something a really lovely to eat, and this is a wonderful rich intense stock and gravy. Please feel free to omit if you don't want to use.

For the vegetable stock
2 large yellow onions
½ garlic bulb (approx. 5 good-sized cloves)
8 large carrots (add more for sweeter gravy)
1–2 leeks
30g dried porcini mushrooms
2 vegetable stock cubes
2 heaped teaspoons tomato purée
*4 tablespoons **gluten-free** soy sauce*

To make the gravy
1–2 teaspoons cornflour for each 500ml of stock
unsalted butter, to taste (optional)

Roughly chop all the vegetables. Place all the ingredients for the stock in a large saucepan with 3 litres water (or enough to cover the vegetables). Bring to the boil and simmer for 2 hours.

Strain, ensuring you keep all the liquid. You can freeze the stock now for use in portions.

To make the gravy, bring the stock to the boil. Mix the cornflour with a little water to make a paste, and add this to the stock a little at a time to thicken it to the consistency that you like. You can reduce the stock down for a more intense flavour and use a little cold butter for a really luxurious gravy if you prefer.

My tip
If you are vegan, you can use vegan cream, gluten-free plant-based milk or vegan butter to enrich your gravy.

Chilli Oil

makes 300ml

We love chilli and I always keep a couple of bottles of chilli oil in my fridge to dress dishes or simply for frying anything including fish, meats or vegetables. Halloumi fried in chilli oil is exceptionally delicious. The two I always have are a strong smoked chipotle oil, very hot, and a more mellow standard chilli oil. It's easy to see the difference as the hotter oil is a very dark red. You can buy chilli oils but they are so easy and cheap to make to exactly the heat that you like.

For a hot oil
300ml sunflower oil
45g smoked chipotle flakes

For a milder oil
300ml sunflower oil
25g chilli flakes

Put both ingredients into a saucepan, cover and cook over the lowest possible heat for about 5 minutes. Remove the cover and leave to cool.

Strain and place in a bottle until ready to use. If you like, you can leave the chilli flakes in and the oil will slowly continue to get hotter.

My Tip
I use chef's squeezy bottles (easily available online, labelled), and keep them permanently in the fridge for use.

Flavoured Butters

makes approx.
125g butter

I find that it's the little touches that people add to a meal that really stand out. Flavoured butter is so easy to make and you can go wild with flavours. I have given you three of my favourites here. Simply melt over any dish to add that extra flavour bomb.

For each portion of butter I use about 125g of room temperature unsalted butter. Whisk the butter for about 5 minutes, until doubled in size and a light creamy colour.

Garlic and Herb Butter

125g butter, whipped
2 garlic cloves, very finely minced
3g parsley, finely chopped, plus
  extra to garnish
sea salt

Mix or whisk the butter, garlic and parsley together. Serve with a sprinkle of sea salt and a little of the chopped parsley sprinkled over.

Sun-dried Tomato and Black
  Garlic Butter

125g unsalted butter, whipped
2 black garlic cloves, mashed
  to a pulp
3–4 sun-dried tomatoes, finely
  chopped (keep a little to serve)
black pepper, to serve

Mix all the ingredients together and serve sprinkled with a little black pepper and chopped sun-dried tomato.

Mushroom Butter

125g unsalted butter, whipped, plus
  1 teaspoon butter for frying
4 chestnut or white mushrooms,
  finely grated
sprig of fresh thyme leaves, picked
sea salt, to serve

In a small pan, gently heat the teaspoon of butter and fry off the mushroom and thyme for about 1–2 minutes, until there is no moisture left in the mushrooms. Leave to cool.

Add the cooled mushroom to the 125g whipped butter and mix together. Sprinkle over a little sea salt to serve.

....index

218

Coeliac UK is the charity for people who need to live without gluten. They provide independent, trustworthy advice and support, strive for better gluten-free food to be more widely available, and fund crucial research to manage the impacts of gluten and find answers to coeliac disease.

Living a strict lifelong gluten-free diet due to coeliac disease, or another medical condition, can be challenging. Coeliac UK can give you the resources and support to get on the right track and be able to shop, cook, travel and eat out with confidence.

Understanding coeliac disease

The charity can help you understand whether your symptoms may be coeliac disease. Coeliac disease is a serious autoimmune disease where the body's immune system attacks its own tissues when you eat gluten. This causes damage to the lining of the gut and means that the body can't properly absorb nutrients from food. Coeliac disease is not an allergy or food intolerance; the only treatment for it is a strict gluten-free diet for life.

Coeliac disease symptoms

Everyone is different, but if you have coeliac disease the most common symptoms you can get when you eat gluten are:

- stomach pain
- frequent bouts of diarrhoea or loose stools
- nausea, feeling sick and vomiting
- lots of gas and bloating
- feeling tired all the time, ongoing fatigue
- anaemia (you would be told if you're anaemic following a blood test)
- mouth ulcers
- constipation

There is a skin condition linked to coeliac disease called dermatitis herpetiformis and symptoms include red raised patches on the skin and severe itching and stinging.

If you are experiencing symptoms when eating foods that contain wheat, barley, rye or oats and think you have a sensitivity to gluten, it's important to first rule out coeliac disease.

Getting diagnosed

If you're concerned about coeliac disease, you can take Coeliac UK's online assessment at isitcoeliacdisease.org.uk. This short three minute questionnaire will help you understand if you should be tested for coeliac disease, providing a yes or no result that you can take to your GP for further discussion. It's important that you do not cut gluten out of your diet until you have been diagnosed with coeliac disease by your GP, otherwise you may get an inaccurate test result.

Getting support

Switching to a gluten-free diet can feel overwhelming, but the right information can make all the difference. Coeliac UK can provide you with the tools to eat gluten free, whether you're shopping for food, looking for new recipes, or dining out.

The charity has been instrumental in helping the food industry to embrace the provision of gluten-free food with more confidence and skill. You can search and scan nearly 200,000 gluten-free products on their Gluten Free Food Checker app, and choose from over 3,000 GF accredited venues when dining out with Gluten Free on the Move.

Look for their symbols of choice, quality and safety to know your needs are being met.

No life limited by gluten

The charity's vision is a world where no one's life is limited by gluten. That is the vision which drives their research, campaigning and fundraising efforts. You can help them achieve their vision more quickly by joining in and supporting their efforts.

To find out more about Coeliac UK's membership, fundraising and research activities visit www.coeliac.org.uk

about the author

Since winning *MasterChef* in 2016, Jane has focused on her love of gluten-free cooking. Her first book, *Hassle Free, Gluten Free*, was published in conjunction with Coeliac UK and illustrates her real passion to make everyday family recipes accessible for all who need to be gluten free. In 2020, Jane was appointed an official Coeliac UK Ambassador and she works closely with the charity to help raise awareness of coeliac disease.

She has continued to test and improve her cookery skills by working with a number of amazing chefs at their restaurants across the UK, including Marcus Wareing, Atul Kochhar, Jason Atherton, Michel Roux Jr and Michael O'Hare.

Jane presents at food and drink shows around the UK, such as BBC Good Food, Foodies, Ideal Home and many others. Her travels have taken her from Edinburgh to Brighton and everywhere in-between, and on the way, she has learnt that she has a love of presenting her recipes and chatting to people about food. Jane has appeared on numerous programmes, including *BBC Breakfast*, *Loose Women* and *Woman's Hour*.

Whatever work throws her way, first and foremost Jane is still a mum for her four children. Some of them have left home, some have boomeranged back with a partner, but she continues to cook every day for her family. Like most mums, Jane is busy balancing work and life and it is this juggle that she channels into her cooking so that others wanting to cook gluten free can follow in her footsteps and make it as hassle free as possible.

Jane also continues to support those charities which are very close to her heart: Coeliac UK, The Ark Cancer Charity, Breast Cancer Haven, RNLI and others. Jane also works closely with local schools to share her enthusiasm for food amongst the students.

www.janecdevonshire.com

acknowledgements

To my wonderful agent Anne; you are a star, thank you.

All the team at Absolute for putting up with my slightly chaotic way of putting a book together and just being so lovely to work with.

And most importantly, my husband Mark; I love you loads xxxx

credits

Publisher Jon Croft
Commissioning Editor Meg Boas
Senior Editor Emily North
Art Direction Marie O'Shepherd and Matt Inwood
Designers Marie O'Shepherd and Anika Schulze
Cover Designers Anika Schulze and Peter Moffat
Photographer Mike Cooper
Photographer's Assistant Martin Allen
Image Editing Ben Allen
Production Controller Laura Brodie
Food Stylist Lincoln Jefferson and Jane Devonshire
Copyeditor Margaret Haynes
Proofreader Grace Paul
Indexer Zoe Ross
Cover outfit Phase Eight

BLOOMSBURY ABSOLUTE
Bloomsbury Publishing Plc
50 Bedford Square, London, WC1B 3DP, UK

BLOOMSBURY, BLOOMSBURY ABSOLUTE, the Diana logo and the
Absolute Press logo are trademarks of Bloomsbury Publishing Plc

First published in Great Britain in 2020

A catalogue record for this book is available from the British Library

Library of Congress Cataloguing-in-Publication data has been applied for

ISBN   HB: 9781472974426
        ePDF: 9781472974433
        ePUB: 9781472974419

2 4 6 8 10 9 7 5 3 1

Printed and bound in China by C&C Offset Printing Co. Ltd

Bloomsbury Publishing Plc makes every effort to ensure that the papers used
in the manufacture of our books are natural, recyclable products made
from wood grown in well-managed forests. Our manufacturing processes
conform to the environmental regulations of the country of origin.

To find out more about our authors and books visit www.bloomsbury.com
and sign up for our newsletters.